MW00464628

BISHOP GERASIMOS OF ABYDOS:
THE SPIRITUAL ELDER OF AMERICA

Publication of this book was made possible
with funds from the estate of
His Grace Bishop Gerasimos of Abydos.

BISHOP GERASIMOS OF ABYDOS:
THE SPIRITUAL ELDER OF AMERICA

Edited by

Fr. Peter A. Chamberas

HOLY CROSS ORTHODOX PRESS

Brookline, Massachusetts

© 1997, Holy Cross Orthodox Press
Published by Holy Cross Orthodox Press
50 Goddard Avenue
Brookline, MA 02146

Cover photo: Courtesy Mr. and Mrs. James Yphantis

ISBN: 1-885652-04-6

Library of Congress Cataloging-in-Publication Data

Contents

Gerasimos Papadopoulos
Bishop of Abydos

The Wise Abba of America

Stylianos G. Papadopoulos

Tribute to a Wise and Humble Abba

It is a daring undertaking to speak about a person; much more so, if this person happens to have been a spiritual contender, one who struggled victoriously for a whole lifetime over issues concerning man and God; and particularly so, if this person became a teacher of truth and a servant of the Most High. For there is no greater majesty in this world than for mortal man to be able to invoke the descent of the Holy Spirit and He to descend always and by necessity during the celebration of the Divine Liturgy and the Mysteries of the Church.

Seeker of the truth, teacher of the truth and servant of the truth was the Bishop of Abydos, Gerasimos of blessed memory. Having lived a full life, eighty-five years in all, he fell asleep in the Lord at the Deaconess Hospital of Boston after a difficult heart operation that took place on June 2, 1995. The operation was followed, unfortunately, by a series of strokes which prevented him from regaining consciousness. He gave up the spirit on June 12, 1995, the day of the Holy Spirit. His Funeral Service was chanted on the 15th. In the interim the relics of the blessed bishop lay in state in the Chapel of the Holy Cross for veneration by the faithful. Temporary interment at Forest Hills Cemetery took place on the 16th of the same month and, about six months later, the relics of the blessed bishop were returned to the campus of Hellenic College and Holy Cross for interment adjacent to his beloved chapel, where he had prayed daily, clebrated the Divine Liturgy, and ordained spiritual sons to the Holy Diaconate and the Holy Priesthood.

During his last days and hours, he was surrounded by clergymen and laymen, former students, spiritual children, and also by more relatives than he had ever had around him when he was alive in this world. He never wanted his students and spiritual children to feel that he was tied to his relatives, whom he nonetheless loved a great deal, and whom he assisted magnanimously in various ways, always discreetly.

What followed the falling asleep, at the Funeral Service and the interment of the blessed bishop, was a marvelous surprise. The cleric who never sought official recognition and great thrones, the man who did not want authority because it was an obstacle in his spiritual life, at the hour of his end had with him a huge gathering of clerics and lay people, both officials and simple believers. His Eminence the Archbishop of North and South America came quickly from New York, together with His Excellency Silas, the Metropolitan of New Jersey. Also present were the Right Reverend Bishops Iakovos of Chicago, Methodios of Boston, Alexios of Troados and Anthimos of Olympos. There were about one hundred priests from literally all regions of the American continent. The Roman Catholic Archbishop of Boston, Cardinal Bernard Law, was there with his higher clergy, as were Protestant Pastors, official representatives of the Commonwealth of Massachusetts and a multitude of people.

And all this for an aged bishop who had retired from his Diocese 18 years earlier, for someone who had no authority, who served the Liturgy in the Chapel of the Holy Cross as a simple priest, and who lived as an ascetic in two rooms of student housing that he never locked. In those two rooms an utter simplicity of objects reigned. Only his books and an icon of St. Paul were objects of value. Everything else amounted to nothing at all. Whenever someone would give him a valuable gift, he would find a way to be relieved of its burden by giving it away where it might be needed.

He lived obscurely and ascetically, in the sense that he constantly attempted to remain free from worldly things, from ambitions and all forms of honors. And while he lived this way without glory and riches, everyone knew that up there, in those two always unlocked rooms, there lived a good and wise Elder, a Bishop and Professor, a humble and significant author. Above all, everyone knew that there was a Spiritual Father, who heard the troubles and problems of each person with patience and love, with deep understanding and much knowledge, with prayer and the spirit of God. Thus he had become the Abba of America, particularly for the Greek clergy, but also for the students of Hellenic College and Holy Cross School of Theology. At times of inner difficulties all could find refuge and spiritual help in the ascetic cell of Abba Gerasimos, Bishop of Abydos. This is why it is not at all strange that this person, who neither had nor wanted authority, reigned in the hearts of the people. And he cherished with satisfaction the love and the respect of so many people; this sufficed and filled him. And for this he was always grateful, to God and to men.

The marvelous, balanced and spontaneous eulogies offered by His Eminence Archbishop Iakovos, His Excellency Metropolitan Silas of New Jersey, His Grace Bishop Methodios of

Boston, the Reverend Father Alkiviadis Calivas, the Reverend Father Nicholas Katinas, representative of the clergy, and all the other related expressions of love, confirmed the profound and universal esteem for the person of the blessed Bishop Gerasimos, about whom from time to time and from all directions one could hear, aloud or in whispers, officially or unofficially, the words that said it all: "He is a saint!" And it must be added that he was also unmoved by honors. It is most characteristic that after Holy Cross School of Theology unanimously bestowed upon him an honorary doctorate in 1982, Bishop Gerasimos never spoke about this honor in Greece, nor did he use the title on cards or publications. He does not even record the event in his autobiography. He did not consider it something significant.

What was the personal spiritual journey of this blessed bishop, what elements determined it, and how did he pursue his own "good struggle?" We shall attempt to briefly sketch his journey, with information that he himself left, and with additional facts that we have. (The basic elements of this sketch were delivered as a eulogy on the evening of June 15, 1995 in the Chapel of the Holy Cross at the School of Theology).

Early Family Life

He was born on October 10, 1910 in the town of Bouzi (today called Kyllini) in the province of Corinth. The poor and inaccessible town lies above the lake of Stymphalia on the slopes of Mount Tzereia at an altitude of 1300 meters. There are few fields and multitudes of sheep and goats. His father was Ioannis Papadopoulos, with the nickname Bazdinas. He was a tall and unsubdued man who lived from his teenage years (without paternal support) with his flock in the mountains or in the winter quarters. He was quick tempered, impatient and strict with all things and all persons. But he had a rare integrity and could see far into life, and he was always ready to make any sacrifice for his children – ten in number.

His mother, Athanasia, was of a different character. She was a meek and prudent person, charismatically patient and pious, industrious and dedicated to her family. She was illiterate, but in her soul she had so much love that she could love God and all those around her as well. Her fourth child, Elias, later to be named Gerasimos, received from his father a sense of honor, an unsubdued spirit and the ability to endure hardships. From his mother, in turn, he received the spirit of patience, piety, love and prudence.

The young Elias differed from all his siblings. He did not fight with them, and they, without being aware of it, treated him differently from other children. The same was true with his parents. They rarely had to discipline him. Shortly before completing elementary school his father told him: "Elias, you see that we are many; you will have to go away to make a living. I want you to become a priest. And I will help you." But young Elias was startled and, knowing the town priest to be a tall and erect man, he muttered: "But I am so short!" Then his shepherd father, who had a rare sense of humor bequeathed also to his son, explained: "Priests are not made by the yard!"

His mother's brothers, the Brilaioi, who were merchants, craftsmen and farmers in Nemea, and one a civil servant in Patras, opposed the idea of Elias becoming a priest, and his father relented which was something rare for him.

Elementary School – The Young "Pappou"

In four years Elias had completed elementary school in Bouzi. For Hellenic school he needed three more years during which he had to go back and forth by foot to Kalliani, a larger nearby town. This was more than two hours walking every day for three years. There everyone, teachers and pupils, saw Elias in a different light, without being conscious of anything in particular. It was due to his prudence which made him appear a mature young man, to his intellectual capacity to understand and, in particular, to his disposition which brought calm and peace to the students, shepherd boys inclined to running unrestrained in the mountains. During that time, his fellow students, whenever they would speak about him, would refer to him as the *pappou* (grandfather). "Let's ask *pappou*," they would say. One day a student insisted that what he had written on the blackboard was correct. And when the teacher asked why he insisted, the student retorted: "*Pappou* told us to write it this way!"

Grocer Boy and Clerk

At the age of thirteen Elias completed Hellenic school. It was summer and his mother sent him high up the mountain to take some food to his father at the sheepfold. There the father told Elias that he wanted to see him become a merchant and would now send him to Nemea to work wherever he could. The young boy did not object, and in 1923 Elias went to the Town of Nemea to work. He became a grocer boy at first and later worked as an apprentice to a shoemaker. In 1925 his uncle decided to send him to Patras. There he worked in various shops and, for a longer period, in a forge until 1928.

Novice at the Mega Spelaion Monastery

It was during this time in Patras that God spoke decisively. A friend of his, also a young worker, took him to an evening sermon given by the then young and fiery archimandrite

Gervasios Paraskevopoulos. During this same period he read the Life of St. Alexios the Man of God. Whenever he listened to the preacher or read the book he was simply pleased. He felt something strange. He felt as if everything was already inside him and was just now being uncovered, being raised to his consciousness: love for the Church, total devotion to God. It was then that Elias received the Sacrament of Confession for the first time in his life, and this event indeed marked him decisively.

For three years he cultivated in his mind and in his heart the great issues, that is, what shall he do in his life regarding the Church and God. His own family knew nothing at all. Archimandrite Gervasios, who had surmised a great deal about the significant things happening in the soul of the adolescent Elias Papadopoulos, advised him to study at the Theological School of Arta, but the necessary funds for such an undertaking were not available to Elias.

Meanwhile he heard a little and read even less about monasteries and monasticism. He constantly had the feeling that a life devoted absolutely to God was something that appealed to him. He would not say anything to anyone. Fr. Gervasios had suspected it and tried to dissuade him. He was a zealous worker and a shepherd absolutely devoted the work of preaching. That whole region was deeply indebted to him. But Elias did not delay in making his great decision – to abandon worldly things, the usual joys and the usual problems.

In 1928 at the age of 18 he left everything – work and relatives who knew nothing – and arrived at the famous Monastery of Mega Spelaion He surrendered himself to monastic life without any expectations. He knew only obedience and service as a novice under the abbot and *geronta* of the monastery. He was drawn by the liturgical life. While he did not understand much in the Services or the Divine Liturgy, nevertheless, everything pleased him profoundly.

The months passed at the monastery and the Elder was pleased; his novice was making progress. Everything seemed good, except for an inner-most disturbance, which was beginning to grow in the soul of the novice Elias. There was a growing desire in his soul for a more austere, a higher form of spiritual life.

On the Holy Mountain – The Skete of St. Anna

For months this inner turmoil troubled his being. Before completing two years in Mega Spelaion, he had decided to go up to the peaks of Orthodoxy, the acropolis of monasticism, the Holy Mountain – Mount Athos.

With strange coincidences, which can only be explained as divine interventions, he set his destination for the Skete of St. Anna. There he served as a novice monk under the guidance of the Monk Chrysostomos Kartsonas, who lived in the *kalyva* – cell – dedicated to the Presentation of the Theotokos to the Temple. He stayed there only because it was the first *kalyva* on Mt. Athos in which he had ever entered. He considered it the will of God that he stay there.

His Elder, Fr. Chrysostomos, who treated him very well, was very meticulous with his monastic duties. But he had no special training nor was there anything extraordinary about him. On the contrary, he was of a difficult character. And from the novice Elias a lot was expected. But he did not complain. Elias tried to meet other more advanced Elders and to draw from them like a bee anything extraordinary that they had acquired through their many years of prayer and the practice of obedience. Within the skete, also under the direction of his Elder, there were others who could help Elias learn the mo-

nastic life. In another *kalyva* of the Skete there were two brothers who were famous iconographers and excellent monks. A
little above the Elder's *kalyva*, in the Kalyva of the
Theophilaioi, there lived another monk, a fellow countryman
from Kalliani by the name of Anthimos. He became a great
ascetic and a famous Spiritual Father Confessor, and with
persistence acquired a great theological education by reading patristic and ecclesiastical books. Ultimately Elias was
tonsured a monk receiving the name of Gerasimos.

At the Skete of St. Anna, the monk Gerasimos made speedy
progress in his spiritual life. He developed the virtue of obedience and became very dear to all the Elders of the Skete.
They so valued his virtue and his prudence that they all accepted – except for one – his peace-keeping intervention. His
Elder, contentious as he was, had quarreled with most of the
monks of St. Anna. His obedient young monk managed in
three or four years to make peace among all of them.

The virtue of peacemaker would accompany him all of his
life. It would be practiced as the work of a Father Confessor,
who brings peace to souls that are deeply troubled. This too
is one of his charismas, one of his gifts to the world. Whenever I would ask him what it was that he received from the
Holy Mountain, he was disarming in his response. There he
had learned to believe deeply and absolutely, to live the Tradition of the Church, as he found it and as it was being lived
by all the generations of believers. This explains the form of
his subsequent aspirations, his ventures into philosophy, his
research and broader studies in European and American universities. They all had the conscious purpose of confirming
the simple and unquestioned faith of the monks of the Holy
Mountain, of demonstrating that the serious seeker in high
theology and philosophy must attain the piety of a simple

monk. He often said that he believed and communicated with God as his illiterate mother and as a simple Hagiorite monk. But then he would explain that he studied, taught, and celebrated the Divine Liturgy that he might know more consciously and more deeply the truth that his mother believed with simplicity.

The Need to Learn – Departure for Corinth

All this occurred up to the year 1934, when an unexpected and inexplicable event troubled his peaceful monastic life. Someone, whose name he never learned, sent him a copy of the periodical *Anaplasis*, which had a commentary on the position of the Professors of the School of Theology at the University of Athens regarding the Order of Masons. Their position was neither for nor against. But it sparked tremendous questions in the spirit of the young monk, who did not have the necessary education to judge for himself. There was no qualified person to help him with the agonizing question, nor could he find one. He was pondering over this issue day and night, wondering why the professors spoke the way they did. He wondered what Masonry is and what influence it had upon the Church. Since he could not find an answer, he thought of going "out into the world" – as the monks of the Holy Mountain say – in order to find appropriate people, to ask them, to have things explained to him.

Every monk, and the Hagiorite monks in particular, give very strict vows to live in the monastery of their repentance, their tonsure. They are not to abandon the monastery and their abbot, as a rule, does not give permission, with few exceptions, for a monk to leave.

Gerasimos the monk, who could no longer find peace, thought simply, monastically. He went to the icon of the Panagia to do his prostrations and to beseech her in prayer:

He thought that if it is for his good to leave the Holy Mountain, upon requesting his permission, the Elder must give his blessing directly without hesitation. If he does not give his answer directly, or if he refuses, then this will mean that it is not the will of God to leave the Holy Mountain. This is what happened. The difficult Elder monk Chrysostomos Kartsonas, even though he had no other monk with him and he loved Gerasimos dearly, agreed to the request. But he agreed with the hope that his monk would soon return to him. The fact that he did not return soon created a sense of bitterness in the Elder Chrysostomos, who had the opportunity to see his monk again only after some thirty years, when Gerasimos was Bishop of Boston.

Theological Seminary – Corinth

In early Spring of 1934 he left the Garden of Panagia, the Holy Mountain, filled with hopes of finding answers to his questions. Immediately, his inner struggle was linked with his interest in attending the Theological Seminary of Corinth, about which his brother George, a teacher, had spoken to him. As a monk, he owned little and had economic difficulties – he could not afford to attend the seminary. These were overcome by his father who provided some funds and by Metropolitan Damaskenos of Corinth who provided him with a small scholarship (from the Monastery of Panagia of the Rock of Nemea, where he had to be enrolled as a member of the monastic community for ecclesiastical reasons). There he began a six year course of study at the Theological Seminary of Corinth. To receive his diploma from the Seminary he went to the Seminary of Arta toward the end of the academic year 1938, where the present Archbishop Seraphim of Athens and all Greece also completed his studies and with whom they had maintained a friendship.

It was a difficult and problematic situation for a young, but so mature, man to pursue studies surrounded by children ten or twelve years younger than he. This was the least of his problems. The diligence and the maturity of the young monk created serious problems for the professors. The monk sought a great deal; they offered a little. Often the tension in the classroom reached dimensions of significant proportions. It was only in music that the monk-student Gerasimos had no proficiency. His voice was weak and not very good.

He read a great deal and he listened carefully, but he completed his studies with even a greater spiritual thirst. In the meantime, in June of 1935, Metropolitan Damaskenos of Corinth, ordained him to the diaconate. A coincidence, a divine sign… he was ordained on the Feast Day of the Holy Spirit, and he gave up his spirit on June 12, 1995, on the Feast of the Holy Spirit, just after Fr. Alkiviadis Calivas, in the presence of friends and relatives, offered the Sacrament of Holy Unction and read the Prayers for the Dying. Gerasimos offered sixty full years of service in the Priesthood.

School of Theology – University of Athens

The element of unsatisfied spiritual thirst simply and naturally guided him to the idea of attending a Theological School. He wanted to study there also with the hope that he would be initiated more deeply into the truth, for whose sake he would enter into many deprivations. It is difficult for one to accept this, but positions and official authority never interested him. He did not even care to have his theological degree from the University, which he, of course, received. He was completely indifferent to such things. When someone understands the absolute nature of this indifference, he also understand how and why Bishop Gerasimos of Abydos remained a monk of the Holy Mountain, and particularly of the Skete of St. Anna, while he lived and served in the great metropolitan cities of the two continents and in the great university centers of the world: Boston, Oxford, Munich, Athens.

Given his advanced age, he prepared himself, nevertheless, for the introductory examinations to the School of Theology in Athens. He experienced some difficulties in the literary part of the examination, but had excellent results in the mathematical.

He entered the School of Theology and began with greater zeal to follow the courses which were being taught during that era by such great professors as Nikolaos Louvaris, Hamilcar Alivizatos, Vasilios Vellas, Panagiotis Bratsiotis, Demetrios Balanos, Georgios Soteriou, Gregorios Papamichael, Vasilios Stefanides, Panagiotis Trembelas and Ioannis Karmires. From the beginning, Professor Louvaris became his favorite, perhaps because of his profound thought and thorough knowledge of philosophy, which distinguished him, and which he used to emphasize the value of the truths of faith.

During this same period, other young men were studying theology and had distinguished careers later, such as Dionysios Psarianos (now Metropolitan of Kozani), Gabriel Kalokairinos (later Metropolitan of Thera), Makarios Kykkotis (later Archbishop of Cyprus), Silas Koskinas (later Metropolitan of New Jersey, U.S.A.), Basil Moustakis (author, poet) and Evangelos Theodorou (university professor of theology).

Unfortunately, just as the most substantive courses of theology were about to begin, World War II broke out in October 1940. In addition to all the other misfortunes, the students missed out on their regular studies. For the rest of his lifetime, Gerasimos of Abydos would regret this loss, which he considered great, particularly since what he was doing he was doing for a more comprehensive understanding of the truth. This is why he always valued greatly the service of teaching, the oral lesson, when the professor would attempt, through various ways, to analyze and expand the horizons of learning.

It is certainly not fortuitous that he himself loved to teach, and he loved it a great deal. While, as we said, he was indifferent to positions of authority, he had a great desire, from this time onward, to acquire the qualifications for teaching, to become a teacher, to speak all the more profoundly and convincingly about the simple and certain faith which he acquired experientially on the Holy Mountain.

In the meantime, and even though he did not have an exceptional voice, he was assigned to serve as a deacon at the Church of St. Dionysios the Areopagite, in the center of Athens.

Ordination to the Priesthood
The Orphanage in Vouliagmeni

The German occupation began and everything was overthrown. At the end of May 1941, with the breakdown of the front in the Greek-Bulgarian boundary, he was ordained – although he never considered himself worthy of it – a priest by Metropolitan Michael of Corinth. He now had the Priesthood for which he never considered himself worthy. However, he did everything that he could for an entire lifetime to honor it.

At this point we must emphasize that even when he became a bishop in 1962, he believed steadfastly that the priesthood is one. He believed that the bishop has nothing more than the priest, being only an archpriest, the first among priests. Primarily the bishop has the particular charisma from

God to ordain other priests. The bishop as a hierarch is naturally the leader of the priests, who also celebrate the sacraments as validly as the bishop, once they have received the priesthood, the Sacred Tradition of the Church. It is understood of course that the priests must be united in faith with the bishop, who in turn also has the faith of the whole Church.

Once, when defending these opinions and explaining to me how and why he came these conclusions, he said: "How does the Eucharist which I celebrate as a bishop differ from the Eucharist which a priest of my diocese celebrates? Since there is no difference, we have the same priesthood."

At the beginning of the German occupation in 1942, Archbishop Damaskenos, who already knew and had helped him economically and morally and who continued to esteem him highly, appointed him to be Director of the Orphanage of Vouliagmeni. This responsibility offered nothing toward his profound theological aspirations. Those years, however, were so difficult that he felt obliged to accept the position. For three years, under terribly unfavorable conditions, he cared for the orphaned children – not only to survive but also to experience some nurturing love.

During the course of the war and the occupation, he helped many people to survive hunger and persecutions, while, at the same time, he pursued with his familiar thirst the meager spiritual activities of the period: lecture, lessons, meetings and conversations with spiritual people. Liturgical life with the tradition of the Holy Mountain constituted the strong foundation, while he sought further knowledge that would help him understand those things he believed. During the occupation, he often visited his professor Nikolaos Louvaris. He continued to do this even after the professor had been imprisoned at the end of 1944, because of his participation in the last occupational government of Athens (at the request of Archbishop Damaskenos himself to serve as Minister of Education for national reasons. Among these reasons was the extraction of a promise from the Germans to expel the Bulgarians from the Greek territories in the north.)

Chancellor of the Metropolis of Corinth

Toward the end of 1945, Metropolitan Michael of Corinth offered him the position of Chancellor. With mixed feelings he accepted. He was concerned over this involvement in administrative matters, but being only thirty-five years old at the time he was daring enough to accept the post. He respected and highly esteemed his bishop Michael, who in turn loved and entrusted his Chancellor. Everything was going well, as long as he left most administrative matters in the hands of the secretaries of the Metropolis.

The ecclesiastical environment of Corinth included traditionalists, who were attached to the forms without understanding their essence, as well as certain hyper-nationalists and some liberals. He himself avoided all extremes, emphasized the need for understanding the essence of things, and worked diligently to establish a balanced view. In particular he wanted to be close to the priests, to create harmony among them, to support them, to point out to them that they should not be involved in the politico-ideological battles of the opponents in the Greek Civil War. Of course, he already held the opinion that Communism was an evil not only because it denied Christ, but also because it did not really care about man, and therefore could not help him essentially. But he never justified the crimes of the anti-Communists either.

During his years as Chancellor, when he was responsible

for preaching and writing, he became more conscious of his limitations. This became clear to him in his capacity as the first co-worker of Metropolitan Michael in the publication of the periodical of that time *The Apostle Paul*, where he himself had to contribute articles and to publish, for the first time, some of his writings. It was then that he realized the demands and responsibilities of writing. He had become so sensitive to this awesome responsibility that, even though he wrote throughout his life and kept notes and expressed his opinions on paper, having composed entire commentaries on the books of the New Testament (on the Gospel of John, the Gospel of Mark, the Letters of St. Paul), including short articles on various theological and biblical subjects, only relatively few of them have been published: two complete volumes, a great many articles in periodicals and two additional texts – a book and a lengthy essay – are presently in the process of publication. The rest of his writings, gathered in five large cartons, still remain in manuscript form, not knowing yet what may be publishable.

Seeking Knowledge in Germany
The Study of Philosophy

His thirst for deeper research and knowledge was growing. His idea for studies outside of Greece was also maturing. From his professors, and particularly from Professor Louvaris, he had come to appreciate German scholarship. Ecclesiastical leaders were recommending England or America to him. He refused. He was offered the position of priest of the Orthodox Church in Munich. He accepted. In September of 1947 he was ready. He had strange and conflicting emotions. He had come to know the evil side of the Nazi soldiers while at the orphanage in Vouliagmeni, where he and all the orphans had been forcefully expelled. The condition of post-war occupied Germany was then terrible: poverty, crime and uncertainty. Nevertheless, the professors and the writers who had survived began once again to work diligently and systematically – so characteristic of these people.

Thus the Archimandrite Gerasimos, at the age of 37, embarked for Munich, Germany, without knowing any German. It was an adventurous trip. The occupation forces assigned him to a room and he began his work. It was the work of a pastor to a small trouble-filled congregation with many problems, and a systematic and extensive study of the German language. With patience and persistence he succeeded.

What did he study in the capital of Roman Catholic Bavaria? When he began he planned to study the New Testament. And this is what he would say when asked at the Roman Catholic School of Theology at the university. In fact, however, he had spent more time studying Greek philosophy. He considered it essential to learn how the philosophers thought about the great questions of man – especially about the question of God. He was fascinated beyond imagination by these questions, and he would be constantly testing whatever it was they were seeking, attempting, and devising. It was clear that inquisitive spirit was still unsatisfied.

All of these questions, immersed as he was in the Greek philosophers and especially Plato and Aristotle, inspired him and he appreciated them greatly. He appreciated this philosophical thinking so much so that he characterized an element of it as a *propaedeia* to Christianity. This is why his first book, the product of research of that period in Germany until the Spring of 1951, was given the title: *Greek Philosophy as Propaideia to Christianity*. This work was published in Athens in 1954.

Toward this direction in his thought, he was influenced by

the famous Romano Guardini, who theologized while philosophizing and created literature while speaking. Literature appears to have never drawn the attention of Gerasimos of Abydos. However, to theologize by following the successes or failures of philosophy interested him a great deal. It was something like an exercise for him to comprehend more deeply the truths of faith, which philosophy did not possess. This approach and point of view has something that is wisely contradictory. But he insisted until the end of his life that philosophy actually helped him. And this despite the fact that all of his writings after 1954 do not show that he indeed was helped by philosophy. Everything clearly constitutes a deeper penetration into the revealed truth of Sacred Scripture and Tradition. How philosophy actually helped him is known only to him.

If we were to risk an interpretation of this fact, we would say the following: Gerasimos of Abydos, through his virtue of love and understanding for people, was able to appreciate any obscure or undeveloped formulations of the philosophers about God and man, in comparison to the truth, and as a spiritual man could show condescension for the failures of philosophers. Such failures, however, were for him occasions to marvel all the more the faith and the tradition which he had lived on the Holy Mountain. Moreover, he would always understand the historical journey of mankind, as well as divine economy itself, as a unified whole, in which he indirectly if not in *expressis verbis* included Greek philosophy. The intense and often successful – in minor issues – involvement of Greek philosophy with the great questions (something which had not yet been consciously and so deeply accomplished in world history) constituted a sort of preparation for man to come before the revelatory work of God and particularly that of the Incarnation. More concretely, he would emphasize throughout his life that we owe to philosophy our thirst for something higher, more sublime. It was philosophy that created in us the desire and brought us "thirsty" up to the point of the coming of Christ. And thirsty as we were, we "drank" from the living water of Christ and accepted Him.

Greece or America?

The sojourn in Germany was coming to an end. It was Spring of 1951 when the first invitations – completely unexpected – reached him to consider going to America. Metropolitan Michael was now Archbishop of North and South America and he wanted to have his former Chancellor, Gerasimos Papadopoulos, by his side. But things did not go well at first.

He went first to Greece, where strong ecclesiastical personalities, such as Metropolitan Agathonikos of Kalavrita and Aigialeias, Metropolitan Prokopios of Corinth and others, wanted him to stay in Greece, promising to make him a metropolitan. While certainly not scornful of this latter prospect, he was not much moved by it. The then Archbishop Spyridon offered him the position of spiritual father at the large student dormitory of *Apostolike Diakonia*.

He accepted this responsibility, which lasted for only one academic year, but this proved to be a wonderful year for the students. In most such religious programs at this time, a spirit of moralism prevailed. Archimandrite Gerasimos Papadopoulos, however, was kindling in the souls of the students a love for Christ and opening their wings for flights into the life of the Spirit. He believed most steadfastly that the opening of the wings of the students had the greatest significance. He believed that with outstretched wings they could fly and find their way, even with some diversions they would reach their goal, they would mature, they would experience the true Christ. On the contrary, without wings at all, or with folded wings, they would never be able to fly; they would remain spiritually weak and immature infants throughout their lives. And if I have understood him correctly, it is in this that the deeper reason lies for encouraging the students then to study and pay attention to the teaching of Louvaris. While disagreeing with him on many points, he nevertheless appreciated how his writings helped the students to spread their intellectual wings. He broadened, rather than narrowed, the ways of the Spirit. He appreciated his work as the spiritual father of the students and had determined to stay in Greece.

America – Holy Cross School of Theology

Once again America beckoned. Archbishop Michael had not been disappointed. He sent a bishop to convince Gerasimos to come to America. He relented and accepted the invitation. Various communities were considered for him in some of the larger American cities. Fortunately these proposals were not successful and Archbishop Michael appointed him to be Professor of New Testament and chaplain at Holy Cross School of Theology in Boston, near some of the greatest universities of America.

By July of 1952 he was in Boston. He had to prepare himself systematically. He worked most diligently in a super-human manner, doing research and preparing texts for the students to study. They in turn were not always well equipped and the work of teaching them was very difficult. He had no time, after all, for extensive scholastic literary, historical and critical analyses. He had to concentrate on the necessary, the basic, the essential elements. This was in harmony with his own character. He therefore drew and concentrated the interest of the students upon the presuppositions, the goal, the thought, the theology of the New Testament writings. The end result of this effort was the ease and depth of movement within the whole realm of the New Testament.

Many of the proposals of the liberal interpreters of Protestantism he considered to be immature things. Once when they told him that Bultmann supported that the original order of the chapters in the Gospel of St. John was different, he responded like this: "We cannot prove that the order was originally different. Bultmann supports another order of the chapters simply because with that order he understands John better and thus would have preferred the Gospel to have been written in that order." Such forms of criticism and the questions raised about Sacred Scripture by many liberal scholars tend to deny something in Scripture, rather than to help man to understand more deeply the truth.

In the area of criticism he did not negate everything. For example, he agreed that a particular saying of the Lord could have been uttered originally in a somewhat different form. He believed, however, that for the Evangelist to record it, it was certainly uttered by the Lord and it constituted an essential aspect of the faith and the Tradition of the Church. It is a revelation. He attempted to comprehend revelation for himself and to make it understandable for the students by also using reason, to a certain degree. He held that Christian Faith possesses an inner logic and consequence which must be comprehensible. It was not an easy matter, yet he pushed on in that direction as much as he could, as much as it was permitted, after all, by the truth that is inexhaustible for us. As soon as he would reach the ends of logic or of his own capabilities, he would surrender himself completely to the declaration of

Scripture, to its straight forward theology, to the "so it is written." Any fantastic creation of new truths, that is, of another Christ, or a denial and a falsification of what we have in Scripture constitute a heresy. He only sought to go deeper into the divine truths, to attempt to know more profoundly the truths of Scripture. This is what he considered to be the goal of the exegete and of the theologian.

He believed, however, that the exegetes and the theologians have difficulties in understanding the truth, primarily because we do not live as much as we should the life of Christ. If we surrender to Christ, then the Holy Spirit "will guide you (us) into all the truth" (Jn. 16.13-15).

Father "ΓΚΑΠ"

His life at the Holy Cross School of Theology was not without difficulties. The spirit that motivated him was different from the spirit of the Dean, Fr. Ezekiel Tsoukalas, who had the unfortunate inspiration to name him sub-dean of the School. The conflicts were many. Archimandrite Professor Gerasimos refused to oppress the students through the school program. He confronted them with a different spirit. He would convince them to work, but freely, uncoerced. And the students would respond accordingly. They came to more than love Gerasimos, who quickly came to be known in the code language of the students as Fr. "ΓΚΑΠ" - the initial letters for Γεράσιμος, Κατανόηση, Ἀγάπη, Πίστη (Gerasimos, Understanding, Love, Faith). These were the perennial issues he discussed with them, and that's why they had become his code name for many years.

With every opportunity and particularly at night his room would fill with students. There were never enough chairs and they would sit on the floor and in the hall. They made inquir-

ies, carried on discussions, listened and were satisfied with
much love and learning. It was what these young men were
seeking, particularly in this situation, who would in two or
three years be ordained into the priesthood.

He lived for the students, no more no less. He worked to
acquire knowledge and he prayed for God to give him perseverance. Thus he overcame the crises and the disappointments
coming from the Dean, who reached the point of first depriv-
ing him of his position as Sub-dean and then asking for his
removal from the School. The Dean did not succeed in his
latter plan, much to the delight of the students, who lost no
opportunity to express their esteem and devotion for their
professor, Fr. ΓΚΑΠ. This reaction served as the highest form
of consolation for the professor, who found perseverance and
persistence to continue the work of teaching and nurturing
spiritually the students to the best of his ability.

During his tenure at Holy Cross it was necessary to teach
courses beyond his own field and to undertake even the entire administration of the School, as Acting Dean, which he
did not particularly like.

Service to the Orthodox of America

His popularity, which was simultaneously scientific and
spiritual, passed beyond the boundaries of Holy Cross. Very
soon he was invited and in demand for lectures, homilies,
and director of retreat discussions in various cities of the
United States.

He gave particular attention himself to the New England
Federation of Orthodox Students. It was the first environment,
outside of the School, where he had been invited to confront
certain critical issues - theological and social - but in a different manner than the one he had been exposed to at the

University of Athens and later of Munich. Here the interests of the students, who came from various university schools, were of a more general character and were not contained strictly within the realm of theological subjects. The need to respond to such demands required him to be initiated into and to become conscious of the intense concerns of the people of the new world.

These critical issues had their own presuppositions and, in their external signs, were very different from those Fr. Gerasimos knew in Greece and in Germany. Therefore, the speaker had to acquire as soon as possible a new inner private training, if he really desired to help these young people and if he indeed possessed the necessary capabilities. And he succeeded. This is why he was greatly esteemed in these circles, where he became a close friend of the well-known Russian theologian, Fr. Georges Florovsky, who also gave lectures in these same circles. This was only the beginning of his activity outside of Holy Cross. He extended himself to ever broader areas and to other metropolitan areas besides Boston. This activity often took the form of a series of lectures during spiritual retreats or of a series of Bible studies.

This activity continued until the last winter of his life. He also pursued advanced studies at universities in Boston, receiving a Master of Theology in 1957 from Boston University. This grounded him and prepared him for the spiritual reality of the New World. This was his fourth and final stage of studies, which he continued with youthful zeal until his last breath. Of the three previous stages of studies, the first was accomplished on the Holy Mountain, the second at the University of Athens, and the third at the University of Munich. One must appreciate the presuppositions, the character, the depth and the breadth of each of these stages, if one truly wants to understand their assimilating spirit and their benevolent influence upon Gerasimos, the Bishop of Abydos.

The Reality of Orthodoxy in America

How quickly he came to understand the problems of the new world is obvious also in the fact that only several months after his arrival in America, he dealt with courageous realism the great problem of Greek Orthodoxy in America, the problem of the Greek language. He not only spoke about, but he also wrote about it, and declared openly that if we want to teach Orthodoxy to our children, if we want them to want to come to our Church, and especially if we want them to be consciously Orthodox Christians, we must speak to them in English, but without this to mean that we should abandon the Greek language. He took this position in 1952 and 1953, when no one would dare approach this dramatic problem among the great multitudes of diaspora in America. He favored the introduction of some English in the Liturgy from that time, yet he still insisted until his end that no matter how many decades pass, no matter how many changes take place, no matter how little the congregation understands the Greek language, a portion of the Divine Liturgy, even a small portion, must continue to be in Greek, in the language of Scripture and our ancient Tradition. The teaching ministry of our Church, however, must be in the language of the people.

In order to more fully understand this, we must emphasize something else. In the innermost being of the Archimandrite Gerasimos of that period a real drama was unfolding. He, who had a real passion for the Greek philosophers and so loved their thought, was also and first of all a monk of the Holy Mountain. He experienced Orthodoxy upon its acropolis; he experienced it in the hearts of the ascetics, who lived consciously the Sacred Tradition of nineteen centuries of Orthodoxy. This is how Orthodoxy was planted into his deepest being. Orthodoxy led to salvation. Yet, Hellenism had also profoundly influenced his spirit. Fr. Gerasimos felt the obligation to give preference to one of the two. A violent inner struggle took place. He struggled to see if he could have both fully. It was impossible. He was disappointed and frustrated. The decision had to be made. The soul nurtured by the Holy Mountain took precedence. Salvation must come first, the Greek language can follow. Christian Orthodoxy is first, Hellenism follows.

Hierarch by Obedience

At the end of 1961 Archbishop Iakovos insisted that Fr. Gerasimos become bishop for Detroit. Archimandrite Gerasimos refused for two reasons. He loved his teaching ministry at the School of Theology very much, which he considered to be suited for him and which he would have to abandon. Secondly, he felt that he had no calling for administrative work, which he would be obliged to carry out as bishop.

The Archbishop, however, who esteemed him very much, both for his capabilities and for his spiritual life, did not give up on the idea. Months later, without telling Fr. Gerasimos anything, the Archbishop spoke to Patriarch Athenagoras. On April 6, 1962 the Synod of the Patriarchate elected Gerasimos as titular Bishop of Abydos. On the day after the election the Archbishop announced the news to Gerasimos, who chose not to say no to the voice of the Church. On May 20, 1962 he was consecrated in Boston and would serve as the Bishop of the Diocese of Boston.

Life as a Bishop

His period of service in the Diocese of Boston would not continue for too many years. Certain difficulties in the Pittsburgh Diocese required the presence of Gerasimos of Abydos. As he began his ministry as a bishop, which continued administratively until 1977, he was fully aware of his own shortcomings, those of his flock and, naturally, those of his priests. He never liked absolute formulations, because they did not belong to the tradition, nor were they realistic. And in order to face the problems of the flock in an edifying manner, he followed a traditional principle: *economia* and flexibility on secondary matters, strictness on matters of faith.

This principle he attempted to inspire into his priests, with whom he labored as co-workers. He had regular assemblies with them and – most importantly – he know how to listen to them, a prized virtue in a bishop. Thus he managed to be supportive in their difficult work as priests in the communities, to earn their trust and to make easier the solution of many problems. He did not have the slightest difficulty in saying to his priests that they, in their parishes, are the "bishops." Naturally there were certain disagreements and conflicts. He was the bishop and had tremendous responsibilities, the primary responsibility, and often had to impose the opinion which he judged to be the correct one. But even this was always done with consultations, with discussion of the issues, so that it was not like some authoritative and autocratic imposition.

His episcopal ministry both in Boston and in Pittsburgh was truly successful, since undoubtedly the flock and the priests considered him as their spiritual father, who wanted and could help them spiritually.

He worked and behaved in such a way that all wanted to approach him and to confide in him. All knew that he had many things to offer on all the matters of the faith and the spiritual life. Yet, he never believed that his service was perfect, or that he had avoided mistakes. He considered his episcopal ministry to be a soft-spoken one. He did not try to impose his authority or impress people. He did not change or overthrow any existing conditions. He only wanted to help the people live more fully and more deeply their life in Christ, the life of the Church. In particular, he always tried to show the faithful the wonderful and saving majesty of the Divine Liturgy.

During the synods of the Greek Orthodox Bishops of all America, under the presidency of Archbishop Iakovos, his presence was positive and edifying when he spoke and even when he did not speak. He had the prudence to listen with an open mind and to understand that, in general, the opinion of the Archbishop would prevail. But he also had the necessary courage and outspokenness to express his own opinion and to support what he believed to be correct, independently of any concerns that might be unpleasant. In such circumstance he never fostered ulterior motives nor a disposition to insult anyone.

In all of his activities and various cooperative efforts with simple lay people, with officials, with priests, with fellow bishops and with the Archbishop he always sought to achieve a balance – a moderation in all things – which he managed to transform into what he himself would call reality. This realism presupposes the knowledge of what is ideally correct, the recognition of the limited capabilities and dispositions of people, as well as the pursuit of what is attainable. One who is spiritually advanced is never satisfied with merely what is simply attainable, but one accepts it with condescension, hoping that at least it will serve as a first step for further progress.

Interlude at Oxford and
Return to Holy Cross

In 1965, as Bishop of Boston, after continuous teaching and pastoral labors, he felt something like an inner emptiness. At the same time, he was seeking out great scholars to discuss certain important problems of theology in the New Testament. Moreover, he was seeking a brief period of relaxation, to set aside his pastoral responsibilities for the sake of relaxed theological discussions without interruptions.

Thus, for several months he went to Oxford, England. He visited libraries and attended various lectures. But this was secondary. The significant thing for Bishop Gerasimos, who by now had 55 years upon his shoulders, was the opportunity to discuss at length with many – over ten – prominent professors and exegetes. He was prepared to listen, but was impressed because most of them were also prepared to listen to him. They were not Orthodox, but he was nevertheless interested in seeing how they thought about critical issues, about issues that perhaps they did not care to write about. Within his soul the Orthodoxy of the Holy Mountain prevailed absolutely, but he was prepared to accept some corrections in his thought about the person of Christ and the divine Economy. Most characteristic of his character and the degree of his spiritual life was his great love for discussions, concerning the person of Christ and the difficult theological issues related to the life of faith of the faithful. He did want to discuss other subjects, and had no interest in hearing what one is doing, how another was insulted, and other similar things. Until his very last days and hours, he wanted to discuss with passion only theological subjects, about "our Christ," as he used to say. It is characteristic that in April 1995, after several months, professor and Metropolitan Demetrios of Vresthena, a person he esteemed highly, came to visit him. After the usual greetings about their health, the two bishops sat down because Bishop Gerasimos wanted to discuss and to ask questions. To the Metropolitan's inquiry, "What shall we talk about, Geronta?" Bishop Gerasimos responded: "Why, about our Christ, of course, what else?"

Ultimately, Bishop Gerasimos was not enlightened in Oxford, as he would say, from the discussions which he enjoyed with the truly wise persons he had met there. He appreciated them, he relaxed and continued there, until certain problems at Holy Cross forced the Archbishop to recall him to Boston in a hurry. It was then that he was given the responsibility to be the Dean of the School of Theology, which he, of course, loved most dearly. Later, of course, other problems in Pittsburgh would require his peacemaking presence there.

Retirement

At the age of 67, that is, in 1977, he retired from the administrative and pastoral responsibilities of the Diocese of Pittsburgh. He had asked to retire in 1976. He wanted to find time for writing and for spiritual cultivation. He always considered very little that which he had achieved internally. Finally, his retirement was accepted on June 19, 1977. What impressive coincidences! He was ordained a deacon on June 17, 1935, the day of the Holy Spirit; he gave his spirit on June 12, 1995 on the day of the Holy Spirit.

The news of his retirement, for those who did not know him well, made an impression. He was still at the prime of his life, working many hours in the day, and people did not expect that he would retire. As a clergyman, a teacher *par excellence,* a writer, a reader and a spiritual father, this act of his was also perfectly understandable. And this is why for them the Bishop's retirement was a courageous act. This is why it was esteemed and marveled at from all sides.

Moreover, everyone knew that Bishop Gerasimos was not seeking honors and authoritative positions, thrones and acclamations. But precisely because he did not seek thrones or authorities, he was truly enthroned in the hearts of the people. And he remained enthroned there, where he still is and will always be. In Pittsburgh, a farewell banquet was organized in his honor, and the greetings and farewell wishes expressed that evening constitute a monument of gratitude and profound estimation for the departing bishop. Representatives of the clergy and of the communities, of the national Greek-American Associations, and of the faithful people of the Diocese spoke most affectionately and with great admiration for their beloved bishop. Naturally, of course, the Archbishop also spoke to honor Bishop Gerasimos.

Before, during and after the farewell banquet, Bishop Gerasimos felt various conflicting emotions: What had been completed in his life? Should it have come to an end? What was to begin now? Had forty-two years of intensive preparation and activity as a clergyman received their seal of completion, or would they find some worthy continuity? And what form will such continuity take? He had thought about everything a year before. Now, however, he was pressured emotionally by these thoughts. And the pressure was considerable. Most of all he was sad over his separation from the people he loved and who loved him. His consolation was that a new bishop, younger in years, would be able to offer more for them and would love them just as much. He believed that people ought not to grow too old in these positions.

Immediately after his retirement, he traveled to Greece. He went back to the Holy Mountain. His cell at St. Anna was now in ruins. A thought he had about living there the rest of his life took flight when he looked upon his ruined cell and the little chapel, where he lived and prayed for four years in simplicity, with frugality – a characteristic virtue and mark of his entire life.

At this point I shall describe an incident, over which I had a considerable internal debate regarding whether or not to record it. Because, however, it has been confirmed by an abbot of a monastery, I feel that I should mention it. The visit of Bishop Gerasimos to the Holy Mountain coincided with the feast day of the main church of the St. Anna Skete. As a bishop of the Ecumenical Patriarchate and a former monk of Mt. Athos, a few of the old monks who remembered him, particularly the monks of Fr. Chrysostomos Kartsonas, naturally, wanted him to celebrate the Divine Liturgy at the great festival of St. Anna. Bishop Gerasimos, however, because he had been living in America had a short, trimmed beard. This prompted some of the monks of the Skete to oppose his liturgizing because, they claimed, the people would be scandalized seeing him with a trimmed beard. When they clearly intimated their perplexity over this matter, Bishop Gerasimos dismissed it, giving it no thought at all. He simply went and stood in a back corner of the church as if nothing had happened, and he remained there from the beginning of the all night vigil until late the next day when the Divine Liturgy was celebrated. There, alone, without any distinctive signs, a stranger among strangers, he recalled his old monastic experiences and prayed as much as he could. It is the custom during the vigil of the feast day of St. Anna for the hesychast ascetics and hermit monks, who live a very austere monasticism in poor, isolated *kalyves*, far from the Sketes and Monasteries, to gather silently in the central church. After the liturgy, one of these ascetic monks approached two leading monks of the Skete and asked them: "Who was that clergy-man who stood in that corner *stasidi*?" They explained to him that he was Bishop Gerasimos of Abydos, who had not been permitted to liturgize because he had trimmed his beard. Then the ascetic monk crossed himself and told them: "What have you done? How could you? All night long I could see over his head a light like a dove, while over your heads there appeared something like little devils!"

I verified the information regarding this incident, and when I mentioned it to Bishop Gerasimos himself, he confirmed everything except the reference to a dove, about which he knew nothing.

At first, after retirement, his thought was to settle some-where in Greece. Arrangements had been made with me because we would have been staying together. He even had sent ahead a small portion of his books, since his destination was Greece. Deliberations had also been made for him to teach a few hours at the Rizarios Ecclesiastical School in Athens.

America Asks for a Spiritual Father

While there were many signs indicating that Bishop Gerasimos would prefer to settle in Greece, and particularly in Athens, to be near the libraries, the clear and fervent voice of the Greek Orthodox faithful of America moved him and won him over. Messages would come to him in Greece, in-forming him that he was wanted and needed there in America. I remember how the now Metropolitan Silas (Koskinas) had come then to conjure me: "Do not pressure your uncle to re-main in Athens, we need him in America! We need a spiritual father to talk to, our priests especially and even we the bish-ops."

I too had been shaken by all these urgent messages. But I had not yet understood how much the blessed Elder loved the Theological School of the Holy Cross. He submitted to the invitations of the people of America, but with the understanding that he would return to his beloved School, to teach according to his ability, living on campus but not being involved with the administrative responsibilities of the School, of the Diocese, or any other institution.

Again at Holy Cross
Teacher, Writer, Counsellor

His terms were accepted. They sent him an urgent express letter. He obeyed the voice of the Church. He returned and took up residence in a typical student apartment, consisting of two small rooms. This happened on November 1977.

There at the School, in a truly idyllic environment, on that verdant hill with innumerable trees, many of which he had planted himself and cared for dearly, Bishop Gerasimos lived another eighteen years as professor and counselor and spiritual father to the students. It was for this purpose that he had been invited to come back. In fact, the blessed Elder felt that he had never really left the School, but rather had lived there continuously since 1952, when he first came to America. Of course, he had served ten years as Bishop in Pittsburgh, but because he was always close to the School in spirit, he felt that he had never been absent from his beloved School on the hill.

At the School, without seeking it, he became immediately the spiritual center.

For four years he continued to teach with the load of a full time professor. Later he taught part time and then occasionally. For a few years it was necessary to teach the course in Dogmatics. He used to read and prepare himself with youthful vigor. He took advantage of this need of the School to study more profoundly for himself the Fathers of the Church, and to attempt to transmit their spirit to the students who would become priests in the future and would need to live with the help of the Fathers.

Study and Writing to the Very End

It seems incredible, but in his retirement Bishop Gerasimos would work all day long. Until the very last days and hours of his life, he continued to read and to write, in spite of the fact that since the beginning of the 1980's serious health problems had appeared. A very serious case of septicemia had kept him for days in a state of aphasia. Later, problems appeared with his heart, which were treated with pills and patience. But the rhythm of his work was not interrupted. Even in the summer, during his vacation, he followed the same routine without losing any time. During virtually all of the summers after 1977, he traveled to Greece. And, of course, Greece meant primarily the village where he was born, Bouzi (now called Kyllini) of Corinth, Stymphalia, on the sides of Mt. Tzereia. He would spent about a week in Athens at the most and then he would go directly to Bouzi. There, again, during July and August, he would rise early and after his morning prayer, would begin his study immediately. He did the same in the afternoon until late.

Whenever he arrived from America, he would seek out significant publications in contemporary Greek Orthodox theology, and particularly works of the Church Fathers commenting on biblical passages. He would not only read these books but would also take notes from them, marking in pencil important passages and whatever he considered useful to him. He had read and taken notes from virtually all of the significant works of the biblical scholars in the Schools of

Theology of Greece. Parallel with this study, in spite of old age and the health problems of his heart and his feet, he did not neglect to serve the Liturgy in the various larger or smaller mountain towns. He never refused an invitation. He usually only refused to wear the episcopal miter during Liturgy. And so each summer the faithful in the mountain towns of Corinth looked forward with great anticipation for a visit from Bishop Gerasimos.

During his years in retirement, Bishop Gerasimos devoted much time to teaching, but also to preparation of his very significant book, *Orthodoxy, Faith and Life* and a Greek edition in one volume, Ὀρθοδοξία - Πίστη καὶ Ζωῆ, in Athens in 1987. This is not the place to analyze this work, but it should be noted that it sums up a very profound analysis and understanding of the work of divine economy for the salvation of the world. This particular analysis of the work of Christ surpasses in depth but also in simplicity many other parallel attempts. In this book an Orthodox bishop speaks about Christ and the Church, a bishop who for many years was a persistent researcher, who studied considerably the secular wisdom, who knew well the opinions of the heterodox, and – most importantly – he had been living the truth for fifty years in prayer and worship. Thus, the work presupposes knowledge and personal experiences and is written in order to edify the reader in a spiritual way. Whoever studies this book, regardless if one is a theologian or not, he will be filled with divine spirit and will be virtually incorporated into the Church.

Following this book, *Reflections on Our Christian Faith and Life* was published in 1995, after Bishop Gerasimos fell asleep in the Lord. Another work on the eschatological faith of the Church will be printed in the very near future.

The teaching and the writing work of Bishop Gerasimos drew, of course, the attention, the estimation and the admiration of professors, students and ecclesiastical circles. More-over, during these eighteen years, the requests for lectures and Bible studies in various communities and university cen-ters throughout the United States continued to come one after the other. Consequently, an ever widening circle of spiritual men and women and scholars were able to experience and appreciate the gift of the blessed Bishop Gerasimos.

The Abba of America
Living the Sacred Tradition

But above and beyond all these things that have been re-lated, the blessed Bishop Gerasimos was also something else: he was an *Abba* – a Father. He was a teacher to whom the young and the old would run at every difficulty with strictly theological issues. He was also the spiritual Father, the Abba, the comforter, the counselor. A whole world lived in the School and even a greater one far from it. But everyone knew that up there on the hill, a little beyond the chapel of the Holy Cross, there lived a wise and holy Elder. In his simple quarters he prayed and studied alone and was always ready to receive all. The very certainty that there lived such a man was itself a consolation. The students would pass by his window and would feel secure. From the central buildings and the class-rooms the professors and administrators knew that at any difficult time the wise Elder had something prudent and help-ful to say to them. The pain and the crossroads of life, the falls and the sins of spiritual people would take the path to-ward the room of the wise and holy Elder. Innumerable people, clergymen and laymen and laywomen, placed before him, again and again, the failures they experienced in their upward spiritual journey. He in turn would share their pain, but would also share their joy wherever they had succeeded well. With or without the stole over his neck, the blessed Bishop always served as an *Abba*, as a spiritual Father, as a Father confessor and comforter. And everyone – indeed everyone – would leave his cell always, more or less, strengthened and renewed in spirit.

This work of the Elder, the Abba, was among the most burdensome and most difficult in the life of the Church. It staggers and empties the spiritual man who has profound sacred experiences and who possesses spiritual wealth that he readily offers to those who come to him. (People simply did not come to him who did not possess such a spiritual life). The blessed Bishop possessed such a spiritual life. He had it in abundance indeed, but he himself believed that it was poor, very poor.

This is why until the very last hours of his life he continued to renew himself, to live with prayer and worship the truth, the mystery of Christ and of life, as he loved to remark. This was so because Bishop Gerasimos, although surrounded by the greatest universities of the world, lived with the daily prayer services as a simple monk. These nurtured him; through them he was "rebaptized" and lived. Early in the morning and every evening he was present, as in the old days on Mt. Athos, in the Chapel of the Holy Cross. And he loved to be the celebrant of the Divine Liturgy, as a simple priest, even more frequently than the young clergymen who loved to serve.

It was enough for the students to see him in the Chapel without fail as an old man of so many years to be silently but consciously instructed, nurtured and edified. With or without saying it, they felt certain of the fact: the Tradition lives! Bishop Gerasimos was the Tradition! No one could tell them that the Tradition had been lost, that it was only in the past.

They had the Tradition alive before them! This is the great contribution of the blessed Bishop. This is perhaps the reason why he had to live the faith and to continue his ascetic struggle in America, in "our Theological School," as he loved to say.

The Hierarchical Prayer of Jesus Christ*

Gerasimos Papadopoulos
Bishop of Abydos

Introduction

Man lives primarily by faith (Rom. 1.17; Gal. 2.20; Eph. 11.1-6). Faith resides in the heart, not in the mind. Faith is a gift from God. Man is created "in the image and likeness of God" (Gen. 1.26-27). It is God who first calls us to faith and brings us to Christ. Christ cultivates our faith and unites us with God for eternal life (Jn. 6.37-40, 44-45; 17.23).

The earliest faith begins with our mothers. It is our mothers who plant the seeds that become the first roots of faith in the innocent, open hearts of childhood. After that comes the life of faith that develops in the Church, nourished by Sacred Tradition, Sacred Scripture, and liturgical experience. Sacred Tradition broadens, deepens, illumines and strengthens our first child-like faith. Each life of faith has its own history. The history of faith is the history of mankind. With faith we can withstand the spirit of the world which attempts, at each historical stage, to uproot our faith in God – the living God who is active in the life of the world – without giving us anything positive for the meaning of our life.

In the faith that comes from our mothers and from Sacred Tradition, we learn many things about the person of Christ,

* His final completed work; finished shortly before his death.

about God and man, and about the relationship of man with God – truths which many prophets and saints of the Church and even angels sought to learn (Eph. 3.10-12, 14-21; 1 Pet. 1.10-12). These truths of Christian faith are clearly and authentically expressed in the final prayer upon earth of our Lord Jesus Christ (Jn. 17.1-26).

Christ is at the end of His earthly life. His public teaching has ended (Jn. 12.36), and He anticipates His ascent and return to the Father (17.11-13). He is at supper with His beloved disciples, with His own. His love for them has reached its highest point: "He loved them to the very end" (Jn. 13.1; 15.9-17). He knows that His time has come to leave this world and, through the Cross, go to the Father. The devil has put the idea to betray Jesus into the mind of Judas, and he has already departed the table, to make the betrayal (Jn. 13.30). Moreover, Jesus knows that the Father has given all things into His hands and that He has been sent as the Savior, the Messiah of mankind, with authority to grant life eternal (Jn. 17.2). And now Jesus is prepared to return to the Father as victor (Jn. 13.1-3; 16.27-33). Jesus got up from the dinner table and proceeded to wash the feet of His disciples, in order to teach them that only in humility and with the *diakonia* of love can people be saved (Mk. 10.45). Following the washing of the feet, Jesus conducted the final *mystagogia* – initiation – when He spoke to them about Himself, about His relationship to them and to the Father, and about His ascent to the Father as victor over the world, sin, and death.

Jesus asks His disciples to remain closely united in love with one another, in order to produce much fruit in their mission (Jn. 15.3). Jesus had much to tell His disciples that night, but they were weary with grief and could not bear it (Jn. 16.6). The Holy Spirit, whom He will send to them, will teach, remind and explain all the things that Jesus had said to them

(Jn. 14.16-26; 15.26-27; 16.8-15). Finally, Jesus concludes with a prayer to the Father which includes all that He had said to the disciples that evening, all that the Church must believe in order to live the faith in Christ. This prayer, as it is presented to us, is a divine prayer. It is the prayer of God the Son speaking to God the Father (Jn. 1.1; 17.1).

The eternal Logos and God, who was from the beginning with God and was Himself God, became "flesh" – a human being – for the salvation of mankind (Jn. 1.1; 14.3-16). Now that He has completed His work on earth, He speaks to the Father who sent Him into the world about the continuation of the work of salvation in the world.

The words of this prayer are divine, heavenly, eternal. They speak about us, the Church (Jn. 17.2-4, 9-11). They speak about our sanctification, the eternal life we shall have with Christ when we live here with Him. They also speak about the infinite love of God out of which all things flow and toward which all things go (Jn. 17.24-26).

The words of the prayer are divine, and as divine words we ought not only to read them, we ought to pray them – for it is a prayer of our Savior Jesus Christ – and only in prayer can we comprehend their meaning for us. God always speaks about us, about you and me, in a personal manner, and not about someone else in theoretical terms.

The prayer was given to us in the form of a few notes, sentences. We must comprehend them from within the whole faith and theology of St. John, and of the Church more generally, and not as a mere text that we examine and judge with our own philosophy.

The Hierarchical Prayer

We have called this prayer of the Lord "the Hierarchical Prayer" because Christ, as the eternal Great High Priest, is ready to offer Himself as a sacrifice for His people. He prays and places all things into the loving hands of God the Father. This is the longest prayer in the Gospels. The theme of the prayer is the salvation of the world through Christ and the Church, the proclamation of the victory of the will of God over the opposing powers of evil (Jn. 12.3; 16.33).

The form of the prayer is liturgical, doxological. It has grandeur, richness, sweetness, beauty. It is divine. It contains regular repetitions, and we can see a logical development of the theses of the prayer in four parts. A central idea is the relationship of the Father and the Son, with reference to the Incarnation and the work of the Savior in time, and, more particularly, with reference to the founding of the Church. The four parts are:

1. Completion of the work of Christ and the glory of the Son and of the Father (Jn. 17.1-8).
2. Particular prayer for the preservation of the purity of the Church (Jn. 17.9-19).
3. Prayer for the continuation of the work of the Church (Jn. 17.20-23).
4. Prayer for the perfection of the faithful united in Christ for eternity (Jn. 17.24-26).

Rendering somewhat freely the first part of the prayer (Jn. 17.1-8), we can say that it is a doxology – a glorification for the completion and perfection of the work of Jesus Christ upon earth. According to the divine plan, the Son was sent into the world endowed with authority to govern the whole of mankind and to grant life eternal to all those who believe in Him, those who believe that the Father sent Him, and that His mission is a divine plan (Jn. 17.2).

Eternal life (Jn. 17.3) is for people to know the true God, and they shall know God the Father if they know and obey

Jesus Christ, whom the Father sent to bear witness to Him. Christ, as the only Son of God by nature, is also the only one who can speak to us about the Father (Jn. 1.14, 18).

Jesus Christ completed His work upon earth (Jn. 17.4); He manifested the name of God to mankind that had forgotten it. Those who accepted the witness of Christ came to know and to believe that the Son comes from the Father, and whatever the Son said and did also come from God the Father. The entire work of salvation is the work of God, and it is to the glory of the Son and ultimately to the glory of God the Father.

"He looked up to heaven and said, 'Father…'" (Jn. 17.1). The scene is impressive (cf. Jn. 11.41). The prayer is oriented toward heaven, where we see the throne of God. You and I speak to God with the confidence and trust of a small child, and we call upon "Our Father…" as father of all of us. Christ who is the only-begotten Son, the only Son of God by nature, says simply "Father," or "my Father," and never "Our Father."

"… the hour has come" (Jn. 17.1). The "hour," which St. John has followed so closely (Jn. 2.4; 7.30; 8.20; 12.23; 13.1) is the hour of the Cross, the hour of the struggle and of the victory and of the glory for Christ. This is why He does not say: "Save me from this hour," but rather He says, "Give glory to your Son," at this time. "But that is why I came – so that I might go through this hour of suffering" (Jn. 12.27). Grant that the hour of the Cross be for glory to me and to you.

"For you gave him authority over all mankind, so that he might give eternal life to all those you gave him" (Jn. 17.2). This verse is understood from within the universal faith of the Church, from within the energies of God for our salvation. In the entire Old Testament, God promises to His suffering people that He will send the Messiah-Savior, who will save Israel and will bring new life to the world with material and spiritual

abundance. These prophecies were fulfilled in the person of Christ. Christ knows that He is the Son of God, who came into the world as the Messiah-Savior of the world (Jn. 1.1, 14; 3.14-16). And the Church knows and believes in Christ as the Messiah-Savior of the world (Jn. 4.26; 11.27).

For this new spiritual life to begin, Christ had to suffer and then to be glorified, to be recognized as the Messiah, in order to be able to judge the world and to grant eternal life (Jn. 12.24; Mt. 8.31; Lk. 24.44).

What Is Life Eternal?

"And eternal life means to know you, the only true God, and to know Jesus Christ, whom you sent" (Jn. 17.3).

True life, eternal life, is to be found in the personal knowledge of the only true God, and in the recognition of the only Son of God, Jesus Christ, who came into the world to reveal the true God to us. Christ, who is always in the bosom of the Father, is the only one who can speak about the true God that we might believe and have eternal life (Jn. 1.18; 3.14).

In the experience of God, both God and Christ are known together and through each other. A separate knowledge of God – of God the Father and of Jesus Christ, God the Son – is impossible and non-existent. Without Christ we do not know God the Father, and without God the Father, as revealed to us by the Son, we do not know Christ. The Father bears witness to the Son with words and deeds, and only in the words and deeds of Jesus Christ given to Him by the Father can we come to know the Father (Jn. 1.18; 5.36; Mt. 11.27; Lk.10.21-24). "Whoever has seen me has seen the Father" (Jn. 14.9; Col. 1.15; Heb. 1.3).

The knowledge that gives eternal life is not simply an intellectual concept of man about God. It is the knowledge of faith, personal acquaintance, and communication of man with

God. It is life in communion with God, participation in the eternal life of God. It is in his relationship with God that man comes to know himself and to have true and eternal life. A life without knowledge of God and our relationship to him is not a life worthy of man, who is created in the image and likeness of God.

The life of faith in Christ begins here, in the present life and will be perfected in eternity together with Christ (Jn. 17.24-26). Man lives his life in Christ. As one advances in faith, he allows Christ to direct his or her life. Gradually one ceases to live alone, and Christ comes to live in him. Christ Himself loves through us and prays through us (Gal. 2.20; Rom. 8.15-17, 26-27).

"I have shown your glory on earth; I have finished the work you gave me to do. Father! Give me glory in your presence now, the same glory I had with you before the world was made" (Jn. 17.4-5).

The work of the Incarnate Christ on earth was to reveal the name of God the Father. The name of God is His very being, His nature and His eternal will for the world and particularly for man. Christ revealed God in the best possible manner: with His teaching, His life, and most especially with His death upon the Cross (Jn. 3.16). Christ revealed God as the Father of love, of love for the birds and the flowers, for all of His creation, but most especially for man whom He created in His own "image and likeness" (Gen. 1.26; Mt. 6.26-30).

The work of Christ, however, is eternal and does not end with the limited time of His life upon earth. Christ was sent to give eternal life to all humanity of all eras and ages (Jn. 17.2). That is why now that He has glorified the Name of God upon earth, He asks the Father to glorify Him in heaven with the glory which He had eternally with the Father, before the world was created. Through the Son, God created everything, and the Son was the life and the light of the world, and particularly of man (Jn. 1.3-4). The Son asks that He be recognized as the Son of God, as the Messiah-Savior of the world that He might give eternal life to those who would receive Him (1 Tim. 3.16). Thus the mission of the Son in the world will be successful and the eternal plan of God will be fulfilled for the world; the world will be saved through Jesus Christ.

Indeed, God the Father glorified the Son.

> For this reason God raised Him to the highest place above and gave Him the name that is greater than any other name. And so, in honor of the name of Jesus all beings in heaven, on earth, and in the world below will fall on their knees, and all will openly proclaim that Jesus Christ is Lord, to the glory of God the Father (Phil. 2.9-11).

With the Resurrection and the Ascension, Christ ascended to the Father and is seated at His right hand. He is enthroned next to God the Father, with His human nature as *Theanthropos*. Thus, with Christ, the whole of humanity is also enthroned in heaven (Rom. 8.29-30; Eph. 2.6). With Pentecost, the Church was established on earth as a new way of life, as the "new creation" (2 Cor. 5.17-19).

The work of Christ is now continued in the Church. Christ is present in the Church until the end of time and guides the world toward its ultimate goal – the perfection of the Kingdom of God (Mt. 28.18-20).

The people of the Old Testament were awaiting for a period of time – in some distant future – abundant in spiritual gifts and with better communion with God. This eschatological hope was fulfilled in Christ. This is why certain contemporary theologians refer to the Incarnation of Christ, to the founding of the Church, and to its teaching and life as an "eschatological event." According to this event, the manifestation of the name of God and of His love for the world in

Christ, the destiny of mankind and of the world will be judged. Men will either believe, come to know the true God and have eternal life, or they will disbelieve and remain in darkness – "as godless people in the world without hope" (Jn. 3.15-21; 12.44-50; Eph. 2.14-18).

Here we must emphasize that Christ came to save the world, to give eternal life (Jn. 17.2). The judgment of the world comes upon it by the stance which mankind takes before the person and the work of Jesus Christ.

How the Early Church Was Established

After the doxology for the work of salvation, the prayer of Jesus is focused more particularly upon the Church.

"I have made you known to those you gave me out of the world. They belonged to you, and you gave them to me. They have obeyed your word, and now they know that everything you gave me comes from you. I gave them the message that you gave me, and they received it; they know that it is true that I came from you, and they believe that you sent me" (Jn. 17.6-8). In the person of Christ we see the invisible God. This is the language of the Christian faith. We speak about God and about the work of God. Let us not seek to comprehend the infinite God within our limited mind. The salvation about which the Church speaks is accomplished by the Triune God, through Jesus Christ, God the Son, who became Man and suffered for mankind, and through the Holy Spirit, who abides in the Church and fulfills all things. God the Father has the first will in the work of salvation. The Father sent the Son into the world. The Son was separated inseparably from the Father and became Man, without ceasing to be God. When the Son, separated from the Father by divine economy, speaks to the Father, we can and should have God in mind, in order to understand that the

work is the work of the one Triune God, without forgetting the three Persons of the Holy Trinity who personally carry out the work of salvation – God the Father, God the Son and God the Holy Spirit.

"... *those you gave me*..." There is a dialogue in this prayer between God the Son and God the Father. God speaks and God activates everything (2 Cor. 5.12). All men are people of God. God the Father sent the Son for all of them, and all of them are given to God the Son. Christ is the heir of the vineyard; He is Himself the true vine and vineyard (Jn. 15.1-10). All those who believed in Christ confirmed by their action that they are indeed people of God, they belong to Him, they are "His people." And of all those people who come to Christ, none are turned away, for Christ accepts them all and gives them eternal life (Jn. 5.36-40; 17.2). This He does by uniting them in Himself with God (Jn. 17.23).

Those who receive the word of God and understand that all things given to Christ – the words, the deeds – all come from God the Father and are not human words and deeds. Everything that Christ received He transmitted to those who would believe and accept them (Jn. 3.34; 8.26-29; 12.49). And the believers accepted the words and deeds of Jesus as words and deeds of God the Father; they recognized that Jesus Christ is truly sent from God as the Savior of the world (Jn. 16.30). It is thus, in these earliest believers, that the Church of Christ was established.

Now this is the main characteristic of Christian faith: to know and to recognize the divine descent of Christ and His divine mission for the salvation of the world (Jn. 1.1, 14; 3.16-35; 6.29; 11.27; Mt. 11.3; 2 Cor. 5.19-21); to receive Christ as God Incarnate (Jn. 1.1, 14) and to entrust your life to Christ, to have life from Him, in Him and for Him (Gal. 2.20).

Prayer for the Disciples,
for the Church (Jn. 17.9-26)

The disciples believed in Christ as the Son of God and became the first nucleus of the Christian Church. This is why, after the doxology for the completion of the work of Jesus Christ, the prayer is focused on the disciples who will continue the work of Christ in the world.

"I pray for them, I do not pray for the world but for those you gave me, for they belong to you. All I have is yours, and all you have is mine; and my glory is shown through them" (Jn. 17. 9-10).

For the world that has not yet believed, Christ will pray later. At this point the prayer is focused upon the Church. This is why Jesus prays and beseeches the Father for those disciples who were given to Him, but who do not cease belonging to the Father, since all that Jesus has belongs to the Father, as all that the Father has belongs to Jesus Christ, for He has been glorified by those who have believed in Him and have recognized Him as the Savior of the world. The phrase, "All you have is mine," indicates the equality of the Son with the Father. No human being can say to God: "All you have is mine," even though God does give us all things. We see this in the mystery of the divine economy accomplishing our salvation in Christ. Christ speaks about this, and this is what we have before us in this instance – the mystery of salvation in Christ. In this mystery, all things are shared in common by the Father and the Son, both the salvation and the glory. There, in the mystery of salvation in Christ, we see more profoundly how the Triadic God works for the salvation of the world.

The Cause and Purpose of Prayer (Jn. 17.11-19)

"And now I am coming to you; I am no longer in the world, but they are in the world. Holy Father! Keep them safe by the power of your name..." (Jn. 17.11).

Christ revealed the name of God, the disciples believed and the early Church was founded. But now Christ is leaving; He is on His way to the Father, and the Church remains alone in a hostile world. The disciples have been separated from the world and are committed to Christ, but they are to remain as strangers in a difficult world, where the danger of falling, of again becoming part of the fallen world, is great. This is why prayer places the faithful within the protective love of the Father.

"Holy Father! Keep them safe by the power of your name, the name you gave me." The sacred name of God is "the Being," the "One who Is" (Ex.3.14). God is above every name. The "name" of God means the very being of God, His character and nature, and His will for the world and mankind. Here the name of God means "his active love for the salvation of the world."

"... so that they may be one just as you and I are one" (Jn. 17.11).

Only with unity can the Church hold on to the spiritual heights of its nature, to its holiness, to its purity from every weakness of this world. And unity can only be realized with strong faith in the divine grace, in the love of God, as seen in Jesus Christ.

As long as Jesus was with His disciples in the world, He protected them and *"kept them safe... and not one of them was lost"* (Jn. 17.12), except Judas who was bound to be lost. Now, why was Judas lost? This too was written, and Scripture had to be fulfilled. This is how faith responds to the difficult questions of life. God knew what would happen and He foretold it.

"And now I am coming to you, and I say these things in the world so that they might have my joy in their hearts in all its fullness" (Jn. 17.13).

Now that Christ is going to the Father, He says these things in the world so that His disciples will hear Him, and they too will experience in their hearts the joy which Christ Himself feels about the work of salvation. He wants their joy to be complete and perfect also. The joy of Christ comes from having completed the work which the Father had assigned to Him (Jn. 17.4). The joy of Christians is also complete and perfect when they know that the Father will keep them united and safe within His living paternal love, and that Christ will come again to take them to be with Him always.

This is the nature of the joy of Christians; the world can neither give nor take away this joy of theirs (Jn. 14.3; 15.11; 16.22-24; 17.24). This spiritual joy is experienced now in worship, in the ecclesiastical celebrations, and particularly in the celebration of the Resurrection, where all things are filled with light, love and joy. This joy and this peace is not of this world. It is the joy and peace that comes from the salvation we have in and through Christ, and which, while we may experience it in part now, we will experience it in its fullness and perfection in the future age, when we shall be able to see the glory of Christ as it truly is in all its splendor (1 Jn. 3.2). If this joy and peace of Christ is not yet in our hearts, we are not yet Christians; we are still struggling under the Law for our justification (Rom. 10.3-13).

The prayer of Jesus in Jn. 17.14-16 repeats the thoughts regarding the position of the disciples in the difficult world.

Jesus taught His disciples all the things that God the Father had assigned to Him, but the world actually hated the disciples "because they do not belong to the world," just as Christ "does not belong to the world." Christ is leaving the world, but His disciples will remain to continue His work, to teach others all that they were taught (Mt. 28.18-20). In doing this, the disciples were hated by the world because they were not "of the world," they did not belong to the world. God took them from the world and gave them to Christ. Now their life in Christ and their teaching appear strange to the world. These are the Christians who are born anew by the Spirit of God (Jn. 1.13; 3.5) to become citizens of heaven, a colony of heaven in the world. They do not live with the spirit of this world, but with the Spirit of Christ and for Christ and in Christ (Gal. 2.29; Phil. 3.29).

Christians live in the world and enjoy all the gifts of life in the name of God. Their lives, however, do not depend upon the gifts of this world as much as they depend upon the personal relationship they have with God. They live the present life with the love of God and with the hope for a better life in the future together with Christ (Jn. 17.24-26). Without these three great virtues of faith, hope and love, there is no real life in this world (1 Cor. 13.13).

"I do not ask you to take them out of the world, but I do ask you to keep them safe from the evil one" (Jn 17.15).

The danger from the hatred of the world exists, and the disciples–Christians would perhaps desire to be taken up together with Christ into heaven (cf. Enoch, Elijah). The Church, however, must remain in the world, to be the leaven of Christ that will gradually make into leaven the whole world – to transform the world into the Church, into the people of God. The world must be saved, and it will be saved through the Church, in "the Truth of God." This is why the prayer asks that "they be not taken out of the world," but that "they be kept safe from the evil that is in the world" (Mt. 6.13; 1 Jn. 5.18). The Church must not be deceived by the evil of the world. The Church must be kept safe and unharmed by the ways of the world. It must not be conformed to the ways of the world and become itself a part of "this world." On the contrary, the Church must be pure, holy, and the light of the world (Mt. 5.16; Rom. 12.2).

John 17.16 repeats and confirms the fact that Christians, even though they live in the world, are not of the world; they do not belong to the world in the same way that Christ Himself does not belong to the world. This is why the prayer continues by asking God the Father:

"Sanctify (dedicate) them to yourself by means of the truth; your word is truth" (Jn. 17.17).

The earlier request "to keep them safe," now becomes "sanctify them," dedicate them, make them holy. Only God is truly holy, totally dedicated and pure of every worldly imperfection, but also transcending every worldly perfection. The main characteristic of God is His holiness. It is in this holiness of God that mankind and the world find their ultimate destiny and goal.

Holiness is, essentially, a separation of man from the desires and distractions of the world on the one hand, and his total dedication to the service of the holy will of the holy God on the other. The entire life of man is a spiritual struggle to be liberated from the desires of the world and to be dedicated to God. The Church is holy precisely because the faithful are truly dedicated to God and live according to His will. But this holiness is not achieved by our efforts and capabilities, because we are all weak. Holiness is the work of divine grace; it is a spiritual rebirth by the Spirit of God (Jn. 1.13; 3.3-5), and it is achieved "in the truth" of God, in the whole truth of

God as Christ has revealed it to us, and as the Church lives it today, in its teaching, its worship, and its sacramental life. The liturgical life of worship and the sacramental life of the Mysteries of the Church have evolved from the person of Christ and confirm His teaching.

This truth of God in its totality possesses power to sanctify; it is the spiritual atmosphere within which the faithful are baptized and chrismated to be reborn in the Spirit of God, to be sanctified and, together with themselves, to sanctify the world.

Some theologians place worship and the Mysteries of the Church on a secondary level of importance, emphasizing rather the word as the principal means of sanctification and salvation. Thus, they present Christ as only a teacher and salvation as an achievement of man. Salvation, however, is the work of divine grace in Christ. Christ gave us a liturgical way to live in order to experience mystical union with Him, to be sanctified and to be saved (Mt. 28.18-19; Rom. 6.4-6; 1 Cor. 11.23-26; Jn. 6.51-58). This is the way the early Church lived the faith, from the beginning to the present time.

The mysteries of the Church, given by the Lord and His Apostles, are an expression of faith in Christ and a very sublime form of prayer. In and through these mysteries, the believer most sublimely lives the one mystery of his or her salvation in Christ (1 Cor. 11.23-26). Responsible persons must always develop and present the exalted spirit of the mysteries so that they may approach them with a real "fear of God, with faith and with love," and to experience through them our mystical union with Christ, with God the Father, and with one another.

The Mission of the Church in the World

"I sent them into the world, just as you sent me into the world" (Jn. 17.18).

The mission of the Church in the world is to complete the work of God. Christ belongs in the plan and in the work of God for the salvation and the sanctification of the world, which God loves so deeply (Jn. 3.16). God the Father – the Holy One – sanctified the Son from before the ages, and He sent Him to save and to sanctify the world (Jn. 10.36). Christ sanctifies the world through His Cross, and now He sends His disciples to continue the work of sanctification. In order to continue the work of sanctification, the disciples themselves must be sanctified, cleansed, and prepared to dedicate themselves to their demanding mission. They must be ready to give themselves for the sanctification of the world. This is why the prayer says *"And for their sake I sanctify (dedicate) myself to you, in order that they, too, may be truly dedicated to you"* (Jn. 17.19). Indeed, Christ, the Son of God, who is already sanctified by God the Father and is dedicated to the salvation of the world, now sanctifies Himself. As a great High Priest He offers Himself as a propitiatory sacrifice for the forgiveness and the sanctification of the whole world (Jn. 3.16; 11.50-52; Mk. 10.45; Rom. 3.21-25; 2 Cor. 5.19-21; Heb. 7.22-8.13; 9.7).

The words of Christ: "For their sake I dedicate myself," remind us of His words when He instituted the holy Eucharist (Mt. 26.26-29; Lk. 22.15-20; 1 Cor. 11.23-26). St. John does not make a direct reference to it, but he does emphasize the meaning of the holy Eucharist: Christ sacrifices Himself vicariously for the life of the whole world. Thus, He replaces the work of the priests of the Old Testament (cf. Jn. 6.51-58; 10.8-9). This is why the Church is particularly liturgical in the life of its mysteries.

The salvation and the sanctification of the world is the work of God and a common activity of the Father, the Son, and the Holy Spirit. The Father sanctifies eternally the Son and sends Him in time for the salvation and sanctification of the faithful. The Son, after the Ascension, sends from the Father the Holy Spirit to continue the work of salvation in Christ and in the Church "until the end of time."

Sanctification means the exaltation of man, his transposition to a higher spiritual condition where he can live in spiritual communion with God. The world of unbelief, on the contrary, lives in alienation from God, "having no hope" and "being godless in the world" (Gal. 2.12). For this reason, the world of unbelief cannot understand and appreciate the Church, and sometimes it hates the Church and persecutes it. In the Book of Revelation of St. John we have a vivid description of the Church in its struggle against the world.

The world is not evil and the enemy of the Church by nature. The world is really the creation of God and constitutes the realm in which God works. God actually loves the world (Jn. 3.16) and seeks to save it and to sanctify it. The opposition of the world to the Church must be understood in a "dialectical" manner. The world in general is imperfect "matter," and God through Christ and the Church, through the "truth of God," seeks to give it "form," to give it the "idea," as Plato would say, and thus to transform the world into the beautiful people of God, to make us "conform to the image of His Son" (Gen. 1.1-2; Rom. 9.29; Phil. 3.21). As matter, the world tends to oppose the work of the grace of God (Gal. 5.17), and this is why we see ugliness in life, "monstrous things," as Aristotle would say. Toward the end of time, when the world will come to an end, the Church anticipates a more severe opposition from the world (Rev. 20.7-10). Christ, however, with the Cross of love, overcame the world; He overcame evil, sin, and death (Jn. 16.33). We too, united with Christ, will overcome every evil force with faith and love (1 Jn. 5.4; Rev. 22.5). The Church prays for the world to cease being the godless world that it has become. The Church seeks to win the world for Christ. The world will eventually become indeed "cosmos," an adornment, beautiful, the Kingdom of God and Christ (Rev. 1.6; 5.10; 11.5). This is the hope of Christian faith: the victory, the perfection, and not the destruction of the world. But all this is to happen through Christ and in Christ. There will be some who will not believe. These are the ones who were not attracted by God in a strong way, and they do not belong to the fold of Christ (Jn. 6.44; 10.26). Voluntarily they will remain outside, untouched by the living love of God. Love only invites and calls us into a relationship; it does not force us.

The Vision of the Church into the Ages
The Prayer for the Unity of the Church
(Jn. 17.20-23)

"I pray not only for them, but also for those who believe in me because of their message... " (Jn. 17.20). The prayer now embraces the Church of all time. Anticipating the preaching mission of the Apostles and the faithful who would be added constantly to the Church (Acts 2.47), Christ prays for all *"that they may all be one... just as you are in me and I am in you"* (Jn. 17.21). The faithful of all nations, of all times must be united and incorporated in the one Body of Christ, the one people, the one Kingdom of God, united among themselves with one mind, one heart, just as the Son is united to the Father (Jn. 10.30).

"Father, may they be in us..." (Jn. 17.21). Perfect unity exists

only in the persons of the Holy Trinity. People can be united among themselves only if they are united with faith and love with God in Christ who is the principle of unity.

"I gave them the same glory you gave me... " (Jn. 17.22). The glory which the Father gave to the Son is everything sublime that one can see in the person of Christ: whatever the Son of God, the one sent by the Father, and whatever the name and the will of God reveal; whatever gives life eternal to those who believe in Him; the victory and the triumph of love against evil, sin and death; the inauguration of the new life and the founding of the Church. All of this glory Christ gave to the Church. All of these constitute the treasure of the Church that received the commandment to continue the work of Christ upon the earth (Jn. 20.21-23; Mt. 28.18-20). Christ is not simply the head, presiding over the Church; He is the Church itself (1 Cor. 12.12). Christ is not simply the heir of the vineyard; He is the vineyard itself. We are the members of the body and the vines in the vineyard. The Church is Christ Himself. The Church is the extension and perpetuation in the world of the living love of God through the Holy Spirit. In the life of the Church the work of Christ is realized.

"... so that they may be one, just as you and I are one" (Jn. 17.22). Christ has enriched the Church with glory and power in order that it may be able to remain in Christ. The very nature and the purpose of the Church demand its unity. And the unity in turn must reflect the unity of the Son and the Father. *"I in them and you in me..."* (Jn. 17.23). Christ will be in us, and through Christ we will be united not only with God the Son, but also with God the Father who is already in Christ. The Church raises the completion and perfection of its unity to this sublime point; the faithful become "completely one." In this complete and perfect unity of the Church, the world will know and believe that Christ was truly sent by God the

Father and that He loves the Church as He loves the Son. "… *that you sent me and that you love them as you love me*" (Jn. 17.23).

Only when people see Christians so united with faith and love will they believe that the Church is truly the work of God. Then they will know that Christ is indeed the Son of God, sent by God the Father for the salvation of the world. Then they will believe and have eternal life.

We must be careful when we say that the unity of the Church is a spiritual matter, an inner unity, or that no Church can say that it possesses more fully the whole truth. The history of the first ten centuries of the Church confirms for us that the unified doctrinal and administrative organization of the Church was grounded upon the unified spiritual unity of the faith. It labored mightily for the preservation and development of this spiritual unity, in spite of the various conflicts that appeared from time to time. The doctrine of faith always came out of, and guided toward, the spiritual unity of the Church.

The message of Christ is that God the Father loves us intensely (Jn. 3.16). This love of God for the world must be seen in the love and in the unity of the faithful followers of Christ. It is in the love of the believers that the love of God for us in Christ is reflected for others to see and believe (Jn. 13.34; 1 Jn. 4.9-17).

The unity of the Church, and of the whole world, is the main concern of Christ as He is about to go up to the Cross for the salvation of the world, the unity of the world in faith and in love. The unity of the world will be accomplished in Christ and through the Church. But this unity cannot come about unless we seek it, unless we live and pray conscientiously the prayer of Christ.

How very essential is the unity of the Church, and how

readily theologians attempt to justify its present disunity! Again, we are reminded of the history of the Church during the first ten centuries, and how it struggled to maintain the unity of faith and of love, in spite of the difficulties, or even because of the difficulties, with which the life of the Church had to contend with during that time of great distances and limited means of communication.

The Prayer for the Perfection of the Faithful (Jn. 17.24-26)

"Father! You have given them to me, and I want them to be with me where I am, so that they may see my glory, the glory you gave me; for you loved me before the world was made" (Jn. 17.24).

Until now the prayer has been asking for the holiness and the unity of the Church in history. Now the prayer focuses upon the eschatological events themselves. The phrase of Jesus: "... *where I am*..." directs our attention to eternity. Christ came from eternity (Jn. 1.1) and to eternity He is now about to return. And He wants us to be in eternity also. Instead of using the verb, "I ask," Jesus prefers to use the verb, "I want." He desires to possess those who belong to God, those who were given to Christ, those who believed. He desires fervently that they too may be with Him in heaven, seeing and enjoying His glory, given to Him because of the love God the Father has for the Son even from before the world was created. Before the world was made, the Son was with the Father. He had been eternally destined to be the creator and the savior of the world and to have all love and glory in nearness to the Father. One is the glory of the Son and of the Father. What Christ desires is also what God the Father desires. One is the will of the Triune God, and it is because of this one will that the Son came into the world (Jn. 4.34).

In the prayer we have a dialogue of divinity about the destiny of mankind (cf. Gen. 1.26-27). The desire of Christ, His final desire which is also a promise and a confirmation, is that the faithful will be with Him in eternity, according to the divine will (Jn. 14.3; Phil. 1.23). The faithful will be blessed to see the glory of Christ in all its splendor, without the covering of the flesh which He had upon earth. Here on earth, we see and partake of the glory of Christ only in part, with the eyes of faith "through a glass darkly." Then, the faithful shall see Christ "face to face" (Jn. 1.14; 1 Cor. 5.6-7; 1 Jn. 3.2).

The final verses of the prayer (Jn. 17.24-26) project into a more perfect future after death, after the end of present history and after the end of this finite world. What precisely this future will be He does not tell us. What we actually know is that we shall be together with Christ, the king and highpriest, and we shall be enjoying his great glory (cf. Rev. 21.11; 22.4-5).

Nothing is perfect, nothing finds its full meaning within finite history. The present appears as a journey toward some future, with the hope of perfection. In the gift of the future, life and faith will find their fullness and completion (Phil. 3.11-14; 2 Tim. 4.8) in the Church of the glory of the people of God (Rom. 8.16-21). It is to this glory that Christ invites us in His prayer to the Father, and it is also to this joyous glory that the images of messianic banquets direct us (Mt. 26.29; Lk. 22.29-30).

"Righteous Father! The world does not know you, but I know you, and these know that you sent me" (Jn. 17.25).

The prayer is now directed to the righteousness of God the Father. It is the abiding refuge of faith to appeal to the God of righteousness with His attribute of justice. And this appeal serves as an abiding testimony to the reality of divine justice, as we have seen in Christ. God is holy and just, and He will glorify the faithful as He has also glorified Christ, the only One who is holy and righteous by nature.

In Christ, the world is divided into two groups: those who know Christ and those who do not want to know God the Father in Christ (Jn. 1.5; 3.19; 7.17; 14.10). The world, on one hand, has not come to know the Father (through the teaching of Christ). The disciples, on the other hand, know and believe that Christ came from God the Father and was sent into the world as the Savior-Messiah. Consequently, the justice of God requires that God will glorify them and will grant to them entrance into eternity together with Christ.

"*I made you known to them, and I will continue to do so, in order that the love you have for me may be in them, and so that I also may be in them*" (Jn. 17.26).

Christ is the only one who knows God the Father because He is always with Him (Jn. 1.18; 17.6; Mt. 11.27; Lk. 10.22). He has made God the Father known by revealing His name to the disciples, and in the Holy Spirit He continues to make God known in and through the Church where the Spirit of God abides. This is the reason why Christ came into the world, to reveal the name of God which had been forgotten by mankind. And all this was done so that "*the love you have for me may be in them, and so that I also may be in them,*" as Jesus reassures in His prayer. The whole work of creation and of salvation is accomplished in order that the love which exists between the Father and the Son may also reign in and among the disciples, in the Church. Christ, who is the love incarnate of God the Father for the world, is to reign in the hearts of men as the living connection between men and God.

This is the most beautiful ending of the final prayer of the Lord for the Church, for the final goal of the world. Everything begins from the eternity of divine love before the beginning of the world, and everything proceeds toward the eternity of divine love after the end of the present history. The present life is what we have between these two points of eternity (Jn. 1.1; 17.24). The world was created by the eternal love of God, existing before the beginning of the world. "God is love" (1 Jn. 4.16). This is the love of God the Father toward the Son, "through whom all things were made" and through whom all things are sanctified and saved (Jn. 1.3; 3.16; 17.2, 24-26). The love of God created all and the same love of God saves all (1 Cor. 8.6). And the work of Christ is continued in the Holy Spirit within the Church, which lives with the same love of God, the love of God in Christ (Rom. 8.39), and which, out of love again, gives its life for the life of the world (Jn. 12.23-27; Mt. 16.25; Lk. 9.24). The beginning is love and everything is love. From eternity before the beginning, and into eternity after the end of present history, love reigns supreme.

The early apostolic Church and the united Church of Byzantium, with the precision of the doctrines, with the system of the Ecumenical Councils whereby the leaders of the local churches gathered to study and to solve through common consensus in the Holy Spirit the various issues and concerns of the Church, and particularly, with the spiritual wealth of the worship of the Church, received a clear image of how the Church lives the glory of God the Father and the Son with the authenticity of the Christian Gospel, the orthodoxy of the faith, and with the sacredness of the liturgical life – for, in the final analysis, faith is essentially a way of life, not a theoretical knowledge, nor even good deeds of love, but rather worship and personal communion of man with God.

The micro-problems that troubled the Church in the past did not refute or abolish the system of synodal co-operation in the Church for the resolution of problems which will always present themselves in the life of the Church, which today indeed has reached into all of "the ends of the earth" (Acts 1.8).

Today we have a more developed spirit of mutual understanding and co-operation, and by far more means of communication among ourselves over great distances that no longer keep us separated. The only thing needed is a truly living faith in the person and the work of Christ, the Son of God sent into the world to give eternal life, the living hope for the future of the Church, of the whole world and, especially, of true love. "Faith, hope, and love; and the greatest of these is love" (1 Cor. 13.13).

May the Lord Jesus Christ shed His light upon the leaders of all the local churches to find again the way of faith and of love for the unity of the Church, where we shall be able to live in Christ, and with one spirit, one heart, one voice and one worship, to glorify the holy Name of the Triune God – Father, Son, and Holy Spirit. In this way the world will also see and believe that indeed the Church is the work of the love of God in Christ, it will believe in Christ, and the whole world will be one people of God with Christ as the one Shepherd. Amen.

An Explanatory Note Regarding the Autobiography of the Blessed Gerasimos Bishop of Abydos

The autobiographical text, published here with the title "Recollections of My Life," was found on June 17, 1995 among many folders of manuscripts of the blessed Gerasimos, Bishop of Abydos. At the top right corner of the folder only the words, "My Life," were written in tiny letters.

On the first page of the text, consisting of twenty-nine pages, some of which are double and triple, we find the same title but with the addition of a date, "May 1990." It seems that the text was written then. It is clearly a first draft. The blessed Bishop certainly had every intention of revising his text, adding to it, deleting from it and improving it. We know from personal experience that this was the way he developed all his manuscripts. Furthermore, we have written proof of his intention to revise his autobiography. There is a very densely and poorly written page, with very many inserted notes in the margins. This page, placed at the beginning of the entire text, bears the heading, "Points in my Life," and is dated November 4, 1994. On this page he has proposals and notations about significant events in his life, about his opinions and about personalities. For each of these points, it seems, he had hoped to include something more, to analyze and develop a little more, particularly his opinions and his emotions during the various stages of his life. But he did not have the chance to do this. On two additional pages he made similar notations in English, which would indicate that he was think-ing of writing his autobiography in English as well. This too he did not have the chance to complete. Also, on the last page, the twenty-ninth, there is an arrow sign, pointing to a follow-on page that was not found. Perhaps this pointed to material covering the years 1990 to 1994.

We know that for the two previous years he had worked to give final form to his book, "Reflections on Our Christian Faith and Life." Also, during the last two years, he had been working on the final draft of a voluminous commentary on the Gospel of John. Unfortunately, this was not completed. The Elder himself had said he needed at least another two years to complete this project. Just two days before the crisis in his health which sent him to the hospital, where he even-tually gave up the spirit on June 12, 1995, he had turned over for publication a study on "The Hierarchical Prayer of the Lord." This paper is his final work.

His autobiography, therefore, remained incomplete. And the literary question arises: Is it permissible to publish a text whose author did not consider it to be in its final form? Inter-national opinion is positive on this question. It is permissible to publish literary, poetical and autobiographical texts, de-spite their incomplete composition and despite the fact that their authors considered them drafts, intended for revision and improvement. This, of course, is done with the declara-tion and explanation that the text is not in the final form that the author would have wanted.

We have considered this opinion applicable and have de-cided to follow it. Our interpolations where the text was extremely difficult to read are kept to a minimum and are only in the form of the words. We made far fewer interpolations here than the Elder himself usually allowed us under ordinary circumstances, while he lived, on other texts he had prepared for publication. Because now he would not have the opportunity to judge our alterations to the text, we kept them to the very minimum. Therefore, nothing has changed from what he wanted to say; his style and his spirit were preserved. In a few places we added titles to various sections. These are in brackets.

It is our hope that the blessed Gerasimos, Bishop of Abydos, the deeply respected Abba of America, will not be displeased with our effort. We have prepared this text for his honor and sacred memory, so that Christians of today and tomorrow may come to know him more profoundly and to have his precious blessing.

Stylianos G. Papadopoulos
Athens
June 30, 1995

Recollections of My Life

Gerasimos Papadopoulos
Bishop of Abydos

The Mystery of Life

Life is a mystery. One must enter into this mystery of life to understand it.

In this, my eightieth year, I have stopped to take a look back, to see who I was and where all the years have gone. Eighty years have passed very quickly; yet I can still say that I have not come to know fully who I am. Perhaps I am not yet myself because I am still becoming. As Aristotle says, everything is moving, becoming in this world. And Plato says that all material things "are always becoming and always dissolving and can never truly achieve being."

Man is truly man only to the extent that he partakes of the eternal idea of the authentic human being. Our life is a constant attempt to participate in this true humanity itself. Aristotle said these things – "to use empty phrases and poetical metaphors" (Metaphysics I.ix.13-14) – κενολογεῖν καὶ μεταφορὰς λέγειν ποιητικά – because Plato could not show us concretely which is the idea of man and how human beings can participate in that ideal. Finally, however, Aristotle sought to find the "immovable mover" outside of the material world, the – τὶ ἦν εἶναι τὸ πρῶτον, τὸ κυριωτέρως ἔχον τὸ εἶναι. St. Paul tells us that we are destined by God to be conformed to Christ. Christ in his human nature is the idea of man, the real, natural icon of God. We become conformed to Christ to the degree that we imitate and are united with Christ. But we never reach the image of Christ the God-Man. We are always in the process of becoming images of Christ, sons of God, but "Not that I have already obtained this or am already perfect," as St. Paul would say, "I am still on the way, I am still running the race toward perfection, and then I shall receive the prize, my salvation, my union with Christ" (Phil. 3.12-14; 2 Tim. 4.7-8; Jn. 17. 23). The life of each one of us, and indeed the life of humanity and of the whole world, is a continuous journey toward perfection, because man, it has been said, is a microcosm – possessing in miniature everything the world has. It has also been said that history is a narration of the marvelous acts of God in His relationship to the world. History is the book of God, through which God directs humanity to reach its final goal. And Christ, through His teaching and life, is the greatest teacher in history.

History is unified. It begins with the creation of the world and moves toward the eternal Kingdom of God. The center of this history is Christ. Until the time of Christ, the world waits for the king, the Savior Christ. With Christ the Kingdom of God is inaugurated upon the earth and from that time onward the faithful have to force their way into the Kingdom of God; they must struggle to enter. "Seek first the kingdom of God," said the Lord, "and everything else will also be yours."

The life of each one of us is also a history, a journey. It begins with birth and continues toward the end, the final goal. Not toward death, as some say, but rather through death to life itself, to the eternal Christ (Jn. 7.2-3, 24-26). This is the real life of each of us, whether we understand it or not. This is the

depth of the wisdom of God, who is working for the perfection of the world: for all things are from Him, through Him,
and for Him. To Him be glory to the ages, amen. (ὅτι ἐξ αὐτοῦ
καὶ δι᾽ αὐτοῦ καὶ εἰς αὐτὸν τὰ πάντα. αὐτοῦ ἡ δόξα εἰς τοὺς
αἰῶνας, ἀμήν. c.f. Rom. 11:36, Col. 1:16-17).

Everything in the world is unified and inseparable – time
and history, humanity, and the life of each person. We, in our
weak limitations, separate this reality into times, days, nations, persons, in order to approach somehow the mystery of
life. Life is not a problem for us to solve; it is a mystery into
which we must enter if we are to understand it. And the only
light which guides us into the mystery of God and of life is
Christ.

The First Period in My Life

I was born in a village, in the mountains of Corinth, called
Bouzi. I grew up in the warmth of our family, my mother and
my brothers. My father would see us as a visitor. He always
lived in the mountains with the sheep. He worked to provide
a good life for his family. My mother had all the responsibility for our physical and spiritual life. She was illiterate – in
her time few went to school. And yet she was very well informed about everything. She raised ten children. She did
everything with her hands – something that is incredible today!

My father helped my oldest brother receive an education.
He helped me finish Hellenic School, which was like a junior
high school; he could not offer any more help since he had a
large family. I finished school at the age of thirteen. During
the summers I would be with my father in the mountains.
Once we sat down together and he began to speak to me as
one man to another. I have never forgotten this spot and the

conversation we had. In 1983 I made a pilgrimage to this place.

"Elias," he said, "you see that there are many of you in the family. If all of you remain here our property will not be sufficient to support you all. I am thinking of sending you to work, to learn a trade; I shall help you become a merchant, to live a better life."

I do not remember whether I understood him or not. But in any case I did not object, nor was I upset.

And so they prepared me and sent me to Nemea, the nearest town, in 1923. The parents and brothers of my mother were there; I would not be alone as I began work in one of the stores.

This was the first time that I had been away from the narrow circle of our family. Everything in the town was new to me. There was only one automobile in Nemea in 1923. Even a bicycle seemed strange to me. "A man on two wheels," I said to myself in amazement.

Gradually I became accustomed to town life. I became friends with other children in the town and I did not feel like a stranger or alone.

In Patras

In 1925 my uncles decided to send me to Patras, a much larger city, where I might have better opportunities. My uncle Theophanis, who was the secretary of the Nomarchy of Patras, found a job for me. So, in March 1925, I went to Patras. Before leaving, I went home, gave the 750 drachmas which I had saved to my father, and received his blessing. It did not occur to me that I should have some money with me. I never thought about tomorrow. And yet I was never left alone in life. On the night I reached the train station in Patras I met some children there, my age and even younger. They were living alone, offering various services to travelers. I told them my uncle's

address and one of them took me there – Ypselantou 25 at
Psela Alonia. I marvel now at the confidence I had in those
children, but I had nothing to fear.

The next day I started working. I was about 15 years old. I
was a good worker, but I made mistakes in my work. I
changed jobs twice. It seemed so easy. I began to understand
myself as an independent individual in life.

At work I was always dependable and cheerful. "Elias, tell
us a joke so we can laugh!" my boss would ask me, even
though I was the youngest in the hierarchy of the working
staff. But I was also stubborn, and they called me "a spirit of
contradiction," (πνεῦμα ἀντιλογίας) because I would retort
whenever I did not agree with young and old.

By this time I was no longer under the direct supervision
of my relatives. I was now a free citizen. And everywhere I
felt the hand of God showing me the way. This is how I saw
every change in my life, even though I was responsible for
every decision that I would make.

I was sixteen or seventeen years old. I went to church frequently. I loved the icons, the movements of the priests, the
deacon as he climbed to the high pulpit with the Gospel, the
chanters with their pitch pipes. Yet I could understand nothing of what was being said.

Through acquaintances I had met a friend, about my age,
whose name was Leonidas Voulgaris. He was more inclined
to spirituality than I. He attended evening sermons in church
and read Christian books. We rented a room and lived together as free citizens.

My friend introduced me to the preaching of Father
Gervasios Paraskevopoulos. It was night and the atmosphere
in the church was most contrite. After a prayer service Father
Gervasios went up in the pulpit and began to speak. The scene

was psychologically suggestive for me – I was listening to the Word of God from on high. That evening I received something – two or three phrases from Psalm 85:10-11: "Steadfast love and faithfulness will meet; righteousness and peace will kiss each other. Faithfulness will spring up from the ground, and righteousness will look down from the sky." (Ἔλεος καὶ ἀλήθεια συνήντησαν, δικαιοσύνη καὶ εἰρίνη κατεφίλησαν, ἀλήθεια ἐκ τῆς γῆς ἀνέτειλε καὶ δικαιοσύνη ἐξ οὐρανοῦ διέκυψε.) I enjoyed the idea of heaven and earth in close relationship. The other thing that I remember was the saying of 1 Corinthians 6.18: "Every other sin which a man commits is outside the body; but the immoral man sins against his own body" (πᾶν ἁμάρτημα... ἐκτὸς τοῦ σώματος ἐστιν· ὁ δέ...). These words have remained in my soul.

From that time I went to those sermons regularly, and each time I would receive something, even if it was just a little. It was at this time that I began to thirst for more.

Lives of the Saints [and the Monastery]

A lay spiritual movement of that time was distributing pamphlets on the lives of saints. I cannot remember how many of them I read. However, one of the saints drew my attention in particular – St. Alexios, the man of God. St. Alexios had left his wealthy family to become an ascetic monk. And in one of the suburbs of Patras there was a church dedicated to him.

The life of this saint seemed like a romantic story to me, probably because adolescence seems to be more inclined to such mysticism. The young person is not satisfied with daily reality, no matter how good it may be. He seeks something higher, something special, the holy, the divine, even while realizing that he himself is falling to something lower. God said it: "Be ye gods." "Be holy, perfect as I am." "We have no abiding city here..." Our city is the Kingdom of God. We are in the stadium for the struggle, so that we may enter the heavenly Kingdom through the narrow gate. There the crown of life awaits us. It was something like this that I saw in the life of St. Alexios. Thus, the idea of a monastic life grew in me for the first time. I kept the idea a secret in my heart, just like St. Alexios who also kept it secretly. I only spoke about it with my friend Leonidas. You cannot keep anything a secret from a friend, and you always need a faithful friend to whom you can express the secrets of your heart. The decision was taken rather easily. I would go to the Monastery of the Mega Spelaion, near Kalavryta, and in time my friend would join me. Everything was kept a secret, from my uncles, my parents, my boss.

At the end of March 1928, not yet eighteen years old, I arrived alone at the monastery not knowing anyone. God provided my Elder, Fr. Dorotheos. He was one of the counselors of the monastery, and he felt a little proud of me because I was educated – I had completed Hellenic School, seven years of study in all!

First Impressions

Filled with adolescent curiosity I wandered around to see the monastery. The Church, entirely within a great cave – the Mega Spelaion – was filled with iconography. I gazed at the icons and marveled at the sanctity of the persons depicted there. I had the feeling that the saints were other-worldly people and this pleased my soul. I had the feeling that I was living with them, living in a community of saints. The young person thirsts for what is sublime, holy. His soul is still pure, even though it is not perfect. A little before Vespers, the ecclesiarch, Fr. Kalliopios, was lighting the vigil lamps – a whole row of them from one end of the church to the other. In my simplicity I considered him blessed. Perhaps it was something he said to me, or that I said to him; I do not remember. And yet there was communication with a brother. He appeared to be pious, ascetic and a capable worker. I thought it was fitting that he should be there in that sacred environment.

In the bright narthex, filled with iconography, I saw David, the Prophet-King. He was holding the scroll: Αἰνεῖτε τὸν Κύριον πάντα τὰ ἔθνη ἐπεινέσατε αὐτὸ πάντες οἱ λαοί. "Praise the Lord, all nations! Extol him all peoples!" (Ps. 117.1). The icon is a book for the illiterate. At that time I was illiterate and the icons taught me many things; it was visual teaching. At that time, I had no idea about the place of David in the faith of the Church; but to this day I see him, inviting the whole world to praise God. That must have been the most delightful and beneficial preoccupation of man – "on earth as it is in heaven." This is what the Church, religion, seeks and offers us – the ascent toward heaven. This remains my dream too – that the time will come when all the nations will glorify God in faith and in love. Here or there, may the will of God be done.

After a year had gone by my parents learned, from a census taken of all residents, that I had gone to the monastery. It was said that my father remarked: "God gave me many children, let Him take one for Himself." My mother and my oldest brother came to see me. The trip then was very difficult. How they came from Corinth to Kalavryta only God knows. In this encounter I saw once again the heart of the mother, giving everything for her children. But they did not ask me to leave the monastery.

The Finger of God? [On the Holy Mountain]

At every stage of my life I could see the finger of God. Something extraordinary had to happen so that I would consider making a change. I was by nature restless inside, unsatisfied – but never in anguish. I always had confidence in the love of God and was always pleased in every way with my life. My Elder at Mega Spelaion was very noble toward me. During a difficult illness he treated me like a true father.

In 1930 a young man from Athens came to live in the monastery during the summer. He had been on the Holy Mountain and he described the conditions there as far better. Restless as ever, I decided to leave, to go there. But this too I kept a secret. How could I tell my Elder, who loved me so and took care of me, that I was going away elsewhere to seek improvement. I told him a lie – may God forgive me – I told him, "They are calling me for my military duty."

The lie is the only sin that I cannot forgive in my fellow human beings. In this I was strengthened by the words of the Lord in John 8.44: "When (the devil) lies, he speaks according to his own nature, for he is a liar and the father of lies." And yet I have lied many times, to avoid bringing grief to people who loved me.

The young man who spoke to me about the Holy Mountain gave me a letter to a friend of his named Stavros, who lived at the Skete of St. Anna. However, he emphasized that I should not remain there at the *kelli* where Stavros was, but should move on to Kausokalyvia, where he had other friends.

At the age of almost twenty years, I started for Piraeus with the Holy Mountain as my destination. I arrived at the Holy Mountain on August 4 with the New Calendar – July 22 with the Old Calendar. On disembarking from the boat at Dafni, the port of the Holy Mountain, I had no idea where to go. I showed the letter I had and was directed to a boat that was going to the Skete of St. Anna. We were about ten passengers in all. Two strong zealot-monks, who had left the Monastery of Gregoriou because they were commemorating the name of the patriarch there, were rowing. Their hands had calluses that could be cut with a knife. On the way we would stop to drop off or take on passengers from the various monasteries. A sudden wind blew my straw hat into the sea. This did not bother me, and the monks realized that I intended to become a monk and would not need it. Along the way all the steep precipices, with monasteries and smaller dwellings of ascetics here and there, seemed to me to be holy and sacred; everything depends on how one sees things. In three hours we arrived at St. Anna. Two monks who always lived at the little harbor were frying fish.

From the harbor up to St. Anna is a very steep climb. It was the first time in my life that I had perspired so much. And yet later I went down and up that path way many times without complaint. The first place I stopped was the central church – the *Kyriakon* or *Catholicon*. Again I showed my letter and was directed toward the dwelling where Stavros was living. I knocked on the door and the Elder of the house came to open the door for me. "What do you want?" he asked. "Stavros," I told him and showed him the letter from our friend.

My first impressions were not particularly good. The Elder was not wearing a cassock, only a cotton pull-over shirt; it was noon and time to eat. He was a little dark in his complexion and seemed to be rather stern; he was neither mild-mannered nor gentle. I remembered the words of my friend: "Do not stay there." Later Stavros also told me: "I am going to leave. You, too, should not stay here."

On Sunday we went to another dwelling where the Divine Liturgy was being celebrated and my Elder had been invited. There were fifty-one dwellings in St. Anna and every dwelling has its own chapel with ten sitting stalls. It must have been about three hundred steps that we had to climb. It was the most remote dwelling of St. Anna. Here, again, I received another intense impression of the Holy Mountain. I accepted this also as an indication of the holiness of Mt. Athos. My Elder sang the Cherubic Hymn from a music book. He was not the best, but I came to like him. "If they invite him to chant, and from a music book, he must be really good," I thought.

In a few days Stavros left and I still had his words in my heart: "Do not stay with this Elder." However, I was not concerned about where I would stay; I was not seeking luxuries and comforts. I thought about it a little and told myself: "Elias, you wanted to come to the Holy Mountain. Here is where you came and here is where you should stay." It was God's will that I should stop here. I declared to my Elder that I had decided to stay with him. His joy was indescribable. He had three brothers in the flesh, the iconographers Kartsonaioi, living elsewhere at St. Anna. My Elder, Chrysostomos, lived alone. He was a tailor of vestments.

Sometimes Elders are strict and they discipline the novices under their direction. In the four years I spent with him, my Elder scolded me only twice for some damage I had done. He simply told me: "Gerasime!" I have not had such love and co-operation in all my life. It was a true father and son relationship.

Fr. Chrysostomos had quarreled with many of the monks at St. Anna. Monks, I used to say, do not really grow beyond their eighteenth year of age. They can quarrel over insignificant things – but as children, without deep hatred. In the four years I was with him, my Elder made peace with all except one. My Elder was not very spiritual. In his prayer, his rule of prayer, his services, he was always faithful. Once he wrote to me, with sadness because I had left, and made this confession: "Perhaps there are many things I did not do, but for forty years I lit the vigil lamps of Panagia." Our little chapel was dedicated to the Feast of the Entrance of the Theotokos into the Temple. And I remembered Kalliopios, whom I had first seen lighting the vigil lamps at Mega Spelaion. Profound theologies are good and so is asceticism, but sometimes one can discern a spirit of true devotion in the lighting of vigil lamps and candles, which certainly brings man closer to God. May the Lord give rest to the soul of my Elder!

My Tonsure as a Monk

I was about twenty years old when I went to the Holy Mountain. Within a short period of time I would be called to serve my military duty. It was necessary that I be tonsured a monk before the police sent me the notification to report. I did not have sufficient time to be tested as a novice to the monastic life. However, with the permission of the Great Lavra Monastery, I could be tonsured a monk before my appropriate time. The monks at St. Anna, out of pride, would not ask for early permission from the monastery. My Elder, however, thought that we should go to the monastery personally, to show respect and to ask for early permission. There I made my repentance to St. Athanasios, the founder of Lavra, and permission was granted. Another small sin here again, and I pray God will not judge our actions so meticulously.

The tonsure was held on November 21, the Feast Day of our Church. I stood before Christ with only a simple tunic, symbolizing renunciation of worldly desires, the depth and the burden of the monastic life. I confessed that I renounce the things of the world and that I dedicate my life to Christ for ever. It was a sacred moment and day in my life. The man who was called Elias in the world was now renamed Gerasimos. This was the name of the Elder of my Elder, but it was also the name of St. Gerasimos, who was originally from Trikala of Corinth, which is very close to the village where I was born – Bouzi (today called Kyllini). During the ceremony of tonsure I felt that I really had become another person. This is how we should feel during such sacred instances, even though we realize that the old man is, to a large extent, still hiding in us. Such instances are the stages of regeneration in our life, as are also the real experiences of repentance and confession (the second baptism), Holy Communion, ordination, and other sacred experiences of life.

I had met all the brothers of the Skete of St. Anna, and my Elder had now come to love me very much as did his brothers in the flesh. All three were priests. Whenever my Elder would see me tired or brooding – something that I could not discern – he would tell me: "Go over to the Fathers to rest."

The years passed in a pleasant and joyful manner. I was assigned to be the Reader at the *Kyriakon* and at the Cemetery Church for weekday liturgies, where my Elder was the Chanter, receiving 1,300 drachmas annually. For an ascetic this was a respectable amount.

Again the Finger of God

In January of 1934 I received two copies of the periodical *Anaplasis*. I never found out who had sent it or why; only God knows. The periodical contained the following: "The professors of the Theological School of Athens, with one dissenting vote, wrote to the Holy Synod that the Church had important problems, other than Masonry, with which to be concerned." The professors must have had some reason to write that, even if they had not expressed it as they should have. In the subtle questions of religion, even the formulation – how you express a particular truth – is a very important matter.

For the monk, however, this statement became a great scandal. Thus, the always restless Monk Gerasimos thought to himself: "I shall go to see how our theologians think. What do the theologians say about our faith in Christ?" It became an obsession for me to find out. It was never a matter of getting a higher education or how that was to be achieved. I was not interested in grades or diplomas. I only wanted to learn, to be more enlightened about the things I believe. Much later, in 1956 at Boston University, the professor in the course on Pauline Theology told me: "I cannot separate my religion as an exclusive religion. I believe that all religions have some truth." But I responded to him: "And yet, if Paul were here he would tell us that 'we are saved by grace through faith in Christ' " (Eph. 2.8. Rom. 10.9). He did not respond to me. Subconsciously I believed that everything is from God and that God will correct everything – remember that a monk does not surpass the adolescent notion of an eighteen year old.

I was mostly concerned for my Elder. How could I leave him alone, after such a life of love and co-operation? My thoughts had to remain a secret, and I did not even tell my father confessor. A person always keeps some secrets that can be said only to God, who knows everything and is able to help in all things. Therefore, I prayed to Panagia and again said a little lie!

Three prostrations to Panagia and a sincere supplication: "My Panagia, if it is for my good to go away, when I say to my Elder: 'I want to go out (into the world) for three months,' let him say directly: 'You may go, my son.' " This is exactly what happened. The lie was that I was going for three months. I did not tell My elder the reason I wanted to go and he did not ask me. He was incapable of ever suspecting anything evil; only after I had left did he begin to suspect. Was everything the will of God, or the curiosity of a young monk? This only God knows. Without the periodical, perhaps, I would have never thought of leaving. I prayed sincerely to the Panagia and, with the periodical in my pocket, I departed for what I can surely say was the unknown.

In the World

In May of 1934 I arrived in the outside world. For a monk of the Holy Mountain to be in the outside world means to be outside the Garden of Panagia – the Holy Mountain. Thus, I was a virtual stranger to all, even to my own family. I didn't know just how to tell them my secret, that I wanted to go to school, to the Theological School of Corinth. During Christmas of 1923 my father had wanted to send me there. But that summer the relatives changed his mind: "What? You want to make the boy a priest?" In 1928, when I wanted to go to the monastery, Fr. Gervasios Paraskevopoulos wanted me to go to the seminary and not to the monastery. However, I did not have the money to pay the first year's expenses, so I went to the monastery. Now, eleven years later, I was in the Theological School. My father paid one third of the expenses and, later, Metropolitan Damaskenos provided a scholarship for me. Parents do not consider economics when a matter is for the good of their children. This is a lesson for young people, to appreciate their parents and to imitate them in their life. I felt very uneasy that I had burdened my father with added responsibilities. When I was only fifteen years old, I had given my father all the money I had saved from my job. I loved my parents so very much.

Adjustment at the school was not easy. All the other students were younger than me by eleven years. I was a monk, a stranger to their way of life, even to their reading and writing. Glory be to God, I was able to get adjusted from the first year. I completed my studies, among the first in the class and loved by students and professors.

My Ordination

I was very fearful over my unworthiness to be ordained to the priesthood. I considered then and I consider now the priesthood to be divine. Once on the Holy Mountain, I touched the sacred covers over the sacred vessels on the Prothesis. I considered it a sacrilege and I confessed it to my father confessor. I would enter the sanctuary with sacred awe. On June 17, 1935, on Monday of the Holy Spirit, Metropolitan Damaskenos of Corinth ordained me to the diaconate. When I turned to the congregation to say: "With the fear of God, with faith and with love, draw near," I could not see the Holy Chalice. The Metropolitan realized my state and he did not allow me to say anything else. Then, at the age of thirty I became a priest. I would look at my *epitrachilion* and laugh with myself; next to the revered priests I felt myself a mere lad. And I would say to myself with a smile: "Gerasime, you too have become a priest."

A Spirit of Contradiction

I was always a spirit of contradiction – at work, at the monastery, at school. Many times I disagreed in class with both classmates and professors. On many occasions the time

of the class passed with such discussions. It was very difficult once when a professor stopped teaching the lesson in
class because of our disagreement.

In 1938 our School went from a five-year to a six-year program, after which the graduates became priests or teachers. I
wanted to go to the Theological School at Arta to see what
the professors were saying. The courses in the two schools
were different. In Corinth the courses were mostly basic in-
struction or catechetical. In Arta all the courses were
theological. I asked to be transferred to the five-year program of the Theological School of Arta. The director, who
rightly wanted to be rid of me, arranged with the Ministry of
Education for the transfer. The papers came forty days before
the end of the school year.

At Arta

The School in Arta was on the banks of the River Arahthos,
with orange and lemon groves, which were very beautiful. In
comparison to the newer School of Metropolitan Damaskenos,
this School was warm and friendly, like a family in all things.
My brother George helped me pay the tuition at Arta. The
director of the School was concerned that I might not pass
the entrance examination. I passed. And when I graduated,
this most noble man, in bidding me farewell, said: "You came,
you saw, you left victoriously." The professor of music took it
upon himself to correct the grade of five which I had in Corinth
to a seven, so that it would look better on my diploma.

And so I departed for our family home in Zevgolatio
Corinth (where our family had come to settle five years earlier). That night I didn't have even two drachmas to get
something to eat. I arrived home late and hungry. This pleased
me, and I am proud to have had the opportunity to experi-

ence all things in my life, without exasperation.

Preparing for the University

It was necessary to study for the entrance examinations to the University: Ancient Greek, Modern Greek, Latin and World History. We were in Athens in large lecture halls for the examinations and the professors were there to supervise. I thought that I had done well. A friend of mine, who took his exam in Piraeus told me that the professors there had helped him. That gave me concern. I waited anxiously for the results that would be printed in the newspaper. For the first time I went to the train station to immediately buy a newspaper. This was the first time I saw my name printed in a newspaper; it was something important for me. This is how man is, he needs to see, to believe. Two of my friends did not make it.

I wanted to enter the University in order to learn the faith with reason as well. That was why I left the Holy Mountain, the "Garden of Panagia." At the Theological School I had educated classmates who did not believe in Christ as many monks believed. One of them later, in 1940, became a Communist. I had befriended him a great deal and it was very painful to lose him. In school we often had very serious discussions about our faith and we were in agreement. When we separated he became a teacher and eventually changed. He was strong and could have served the Church well. Unfortunately, during the war he was killed, without my ever seeing him again. Only God knows what is hidden in man. Only God can judge.

I must say that the Church did not understand well those strong young persons who were well-educated, but who lacked a complete spiritual formation in Christ. She did not come to understand them and to approach them with love.

This is why many teachers became Communists, rousing up the people in timely and untimely fashion, with ideologies, with promises of a better life, and more often with threats: "If you do not join with us, you are traitors, and we will destroy your family!" Great crimes were committed, and, as I used to say, if Communism is not condemned by the conscience of the people, the period of World War II will be a stigma for Greece.

The events of 1989 have clearly justified me. The motives of Communism may have had some positive basis. But their method of implementation was anti-Christian and destructive. The leaders of Communism were dynamic, educated, and could see the poverty and the great chasm between the rich and the poor. But they could not see the human being as an image of God. They took man as a tool in their hands, to be used to change the material condition of his life as they had envisioned it. But life really belongs to God and it can only be changed with love, with the will of God, and with our free will and co-operation. The change must come about through high ideals and not through laws and force, with faith in God and with love. I wanted to say something like this at the university, but such thoughts do not derive from the teaching alone; they rise up from the depth of our souls when the heart is moved.

Crisis of Faith

Most of the courses during the first year at the University were introductions to Sacred Scripture, Church History, etc., and as such opened up for me a little the horizon of thought. I was convinced that I had actually learned something. Later, in America, I learned that second year university students are called sophomores! I passed all the courses, including

Hebrew grammar, even if I didn't get good grades. I was not interested in good grades. What I was seeking was to enter into the essence of the subject, faith in Christ.

I never thought about grades and diplomas. The important thing was to penetrate more into the elements of my faith in Christ. As some would whisper, the university is interested in the "science" of theology, not in faith. But the "science" of a Christian school has as its purpose to enlighten faith and not simply to explain certain grammatical or historical obscurities. The thought of the Apostles and of the Fathers that we study had as its purpose the essence of the Faith.

Was I curious, a rationalist, another Thomas who wanted to touch the invisible aspects of the faith? I must admit I was a little of all the above. I was not prepared to accept anything that I could not examine logically. Knowledge which was merely informative did not help me with the issues of faith. Logical thoughts by themselves do not guide one anywhere, or rather, they guide one to doubt, to emptiness, to nihilism; they guide one to hypothetical issues, such as the original eruption, the "Big Bang," from which the incomprehensible world emerged. These thoughts perhaps led me to the first crisis of faith, shaking the foundations of faith.

One day the urgent question came to me: Who is Christ? Why do we believe in Christ? And I was at the time a deacon at the Church of St. Dionysios the Areopagite in Athens. I did not exorcise the idea at first, but there was no logical answer to the question. These were the most difficult days in my life. For three days I was not certain that I existed. The earth was shaken from underneath my feet. Suddenly, while lying in bed, the idea came to me. I saw the civilization of Christianity. I saw the great personalities of the Saints created by their Faith in Christ, and I said: "Behold Christ! Christ is the One who changes all things, who makes all things new! If anyone is in Christ, he is a new creation" (2 Cor. 5.17). At that moment I recalled a serious proverb: "Here is the wolf! Where are his tracks?" It seems that two men were seeking to find the wolf. One man saw him and declared: "Here is the wolf." The other man was still asking to see his tracks: "Where are his tracks?" The signposts which Christ left guide us to Him. And when the heart has seen and has received Christ, it no longer needs to search. At the very least, we look upon the tracks and confirm our faith formally.

The same thing happened to Aristotle. His teacher Plato came to the conclusion about the ideas in order to establish a foundation for the material world. Aristotle called this "empty words," that is, "being in the clouds." He himself does not search in the material things to find the traces of the real essence, but rather to reach himself the end, the *telos*, and to say: "The first immovable mover is outside of the world. The primary principle is that which truly is, the first, the one who primarily has being." Scientific knowledge is beneficial and useful, satisfying the curiosity of the mind. But the mind needs faith as a place to stand within the dangerous pathways of research, where one can lose his way before arriving at the peak, at the essence of things.

The Second World War

In October, 1940, I had purchased a briefcase and was ready to begin the second year at the University. I had been assigned to serve as Deacon at the Church of St. Dionysios, the patron Saint of Athens. How I received that assignment only God knows. On October 28, 1940, Italy declared war on Greece. And eternal Greece responded with the "No" of Prime Minister Metaxas. We defeated the Italians in Albania, but the

Germans came to join in the struggle against us. The women and the mothers were crying. I could see the might of Germany, and did not believe that the war could last very long. The war ended but its consequences continued.

My mother had seen me in her dream, because my brother and I were in a very difficult situation in Athens. She saw in her dream that we would come to Corinth, and that I would go to our house in the family field. "Get up," she said to my father, "our son is coming to the field." Another time, when the front in Albania had been broken and the Greek Army began to retreat, my mother prayed to Panagia to tell her where Andreas, her son-in-law, was. And Panagia reassured her that indeed Andreas is well. How great is the heart of a mother! My mother again, when she heard that we were killing Italians in the war, told me: "My son, are we going to find mercy? They too are human beings." I myself, as a cleric, did not think like that. I shall never forget it.

In April, 1941, the Germans entered Athens. Then the guerrilla fighters appeared, both of the EAM-EΛΛΑΣ (leftists) and of the rightists. Each side was seeking to take advantage of the fall of the country in order to impose its own ideology. For the Communists it was a unique opportunity to prevail in Greece. They did everything with the pretense of patriotism. Never ask who was in the right or in the wrong. Dissension had come and there was no love among our people. This division still holds a grip over our country. It takes a great deal of spiritual maturity and strength to forgive and forget those terrible crimes that were committed. They remain to this day a stigma upon the history of Greece. And many of us who lived through them then, continue to live them still today.

The Question of Military Service

With the declaration of war, we all had to go to war. When in 1939 Metropolitan Damaskenos wanted to send me to the Theological School of Halki, I had to acquire a document saying that I was free of any military obligations. The Monastery of St. Athanasios (The Great Lavra) on Mt. Athos had removed my name from its list of monks, because I had been absent for more than a year. Consequently, I was obliged to serve in the military before I could go abroad. At the time I was a Deacon, and I wanted at least to complete the Ecclesiastical School. A captain in the military, as a gesture of good will, interceded and they granted me a postponement for reasons of health, making me eligible to be called for duty in 1941. In 1940 the war broke out and the conscripts for 1941 were called to go to war. This group, however, did not include those who had been enlisted for the year 1941 through postponement as I was.

Taking into consideration that I would probably be called to duty any time soon, I requested to be ordained into the priesthood by the ever-memorable Metropolitan Michael of Corinth, on March 29, 1941 at the chapel of St. Photine. And yet I could not believe that I too had become a priest, as I considered the priesthood with such high regard. I looked upon revered priests and then I looked upon myself and would remark to myself: "You too are now a priest, Gerasime?" I continued to serve the Church of St. Dionysios, as an assistant priest, and the Archdiocese would also send me wherever there was a need. A friend of mine, a deacon, wanted to serve the Liturgy at St. Dionysios. I had no permission from the Archdiocese. This made him very sad to the point of despair. Out of sympathy I decided to serve with him, in the hope that the Archdiocese would not learn of it. A brother priest telephoned the Archdiocese, and I was placed on probation. Not long afterward, during a certain difficulty of mine, that same deacon was criticizing me as being timid, as not knowing how to function. Perhaps he was right. Thus, I was hurt by two brothers. I did not repent. I acknowledged that I made a mistake, but I did it knowingly for the sake of a hurting brother. Twice in my life I have cried for the pain of others – and such tears have a sweetness about them!

[The Orphanage of Vouliagmeni]

Metropolitan Damaskenos of Corinth became Archbishop of Athens and all Greece in January, 1942. That same month the position of director of the orphanage of the Archdiocese of Athens became available. At the suggestion of Father Lukas, the first priest of the Church of St. Dionysios, Archbishop Damaskenos appointed me to be director of the orphanage. Those years were extremely difficult. But with the help of God we endured and the years passed. I came to love the children very much. In matters of administration, however, I did not have the austerity that was often required and from time to time we had some small problems.

On November 12, 1944, the orphanage was transferred to a building in Vouliagmeni, where up to that time Germans had been living. I remembered the "Christian Corner." I was in captivity here, now. . . . That night I watched the moon, it was magnificent. I made the Sign of the Cross over the sea and the boats, and I continued to look at the moon until its setting. As it left the final ray of reflected light, I greeted it and glorified God. On another occasion I watched the setting of the sun and then the rising of the moon with some friends. It was an indescribably beautiful sight.

The University had to close, and it became the dwelling place for many refugees. It was open only two or three months

of the year. For the three best years I did not have the opportunity to listen to the professors. Even to this day, I feel that
some basic elements of theoretical and historical knowledge
that one acquires in school are lacking in me. In May, 1943, I
completed my studies at the University. In June I took my
written examinations. In December, 1943 and January, 1944, I
passed my oral examinations and then received my diploma.
My dream of higher education had become a reality. I returned
to the orphanage where I had been director and told the children about my life, as a story of a village boy. I wanted the
orphans to realize that they could some day become professors and important people. I cannot forget the final
examinations with Professor Balanos. He told the three of us
– Fr. Germanos Psalidakis, Savvas Koskinas and me – "Con-
gratulations, you have done excellent work, all three of you."
The three of us later became bishops in America.

Chancellor in Corinth

In December, 1945, the position of chancellor in the Metropolis of Corinth was vacated. Metropolitan Michael
preferred to have me in that position. Thus, for the first time,
I received an administrative position in the life of the Church.
I saw the life of the Church from close up: the parishes, the
spiritual condition of the people. The preaching in Athens
and the preaching in Corinth was different.

I tried to have a close co-operation with the Metropolitan,
with the secretaries, and with the priests. I always wanted to
support and strengthen the position of our priests so that they
could enjoy the appropriate recognition and respect from the
people. In particular, I struggled to bring peace among the
priests whenever they had serious differences, in spite of the
pessimism of the Metropolitan. I showed them love and pa-

tience and humility, and with the help of Christ the reconciliation would eventually come. My joy, as a young chancellor and later as a bishop, was to communicate with the priests.

About two years passed. Everything was going well. But in my soul something was missing. After the spiritual encounters and contacts that I had in Athens, Corinth seemed to me provincial. I did not manage to have good relations with the professors of the Ecclesiastical School. For everyone those years were difficult. In my diary in March, 1947, I had written: "When shall I find myself again in Athens to hear lectures and to have spiritual conversations?"

Once again the finger of God seemed to point me in another direction. While I was thinking about such things, I received a letter from a close friend, the Archimandrite Theoklitos Mihalas. He wrote that in Munich, Germany they were seeking a priest. Was this the finger of God? If he had not written to me, I would have never heard of this. And there was another priest from Halki who wanted to go to Germany. The secret is that I was ready for an adventure. Total lack of fear, or rather, a tendency toward the unknown and curiosity held sway in my decision. I left my home for the first time when I was thirteen years old, without even a second thought. I left for the monastery, for the Holy Mountain, and now for Germany – later for America, for Oxford. When I mentioned the plan to Metropolitan Michael, he said: "I shall send you to England." Later he changed his mind, and so we submitted and application for Germany. Others did not even submit an application, being concerned about the conditions in war-torn and defeated Germany.

And what about the issue of military service? The authorities simply assumed that, as I was a priest, I must have served. They issued me a permit to leave the country. I had my hair cut, I ordered two suits and I was ready. It was September 5, 1947. There were many irregularities in Greece at that time. The policeman at the airport looked at my passport. "Have you served in the army?" he asked me. I said "Yes." If he had any psychological insight he would have realized that I had lied. Then he asked me: "Were you an officer in the army?" "No," I answered with relief. If I had been an officer, I know that he would not have allowed me to leave. The officers had to be prepared to serve their country in its time of need. Thus I boarded the airplane and flew to Germany.

In Germany

I went by airplane to Zurich, and from there by train to Munich. I did not know German. I did not know that trains changed between cities. In each city God provided someone to guide me to the right place. Otherwise, I would have certainly gotten lost. I reached Munich at dawn the next day. For the first time, tired from sleeplessness and the anxiety of the unknown, I slept in a chair of the hotel near the station. Early in the morning Mr. Gogos came to meet me. It was September 7, 1947.

My predecessor, Fr. Meletios, later Metropolitan of Kythera, was still there. He had suffered a great deal from the Germans. He too was weary. Together with Mr. Gryparis, a military man, they had found a room for me on Ismaninger Street. The Greeks, as allies, had the right to requisition a room that was not considered essential to the German owners. On the door outside the room was the following sign: "The person who lives here belongs to the Kingdom of Greece." This meant that no one could make any trouble for me.

Hunger

This was the period immediately after the destruction of the war. There were shortages in everything, even food. In the evening, at 7:00 p.m., an unusual time for me, we would have dinner. One slice of dark bread with a little butter and half a tomato that was grown on the balcony. I accepted all this. I accepted the lesson and smiled. I smile when I meet difficulties that I cannot avoid. I had faith in God that the conditions would improve. With the first German phrases that I learned, I would say: "*Morgen wird es besser* . . . Tomorrow will be better." And in three months the situation changed. At the market place you could then find anything you wanted, but at a rather high cost.

Our Church

This was for me the first time that I was outside Greece and the Greek Church. The environment was Roman Catholic. The majority of the books were Protestant. I saw our Church somewhat differently, independently. The church itself in Munich is a German archaeological monument. It was built in 1496 in the Gothic architectural style. It had beautiful stained glass windows, which had been destroyed during the war. The church had been offered as a gift from the Bavarian government, to honor the Greek community and for their liturgical use.

My flock consisted of about fifteen to twenty families in Munich and the surrounding area. They were pious people, but not strongly attached to the Church. The students who had settled in Munich, and those who were still studying there, were the main strength of the community. The time to start the Liturgy had to be coordinated with the time the train arrived from the surrounding area where many students lived.

They were my choir, my companions, my helpers. I was actually responsible for all of Germany, and from time to time, I would travel to other major cities in Germany, mainly for the sacraments.

And What About the Masons?

Gradually over the years I had forgotten why I left the Holy Mountain in the first place. Immersed in my studies, discussions and responsibilities, I had forgotten myself. My desire was to enter into the truth of Christianity as much as I could. It was for me an existential matter – I needed to know why I live and how I live. Instead of the New Testament, which I would have liked to study, I turned more to the study of philosophy, ancient Greek philosophy. There I saw human thought.

It took me a year to learn German well enough to read books and to follow courses at the University. I took courses in philosophy, New Testament and dogmatics. I did not feel ready yet to work for a doctorate, nor was I interested in a diploma. My thirst was to learn. I loved to learn. Of all the professors, I enjoyed Rudolf Guardini the most. He taught theology with the help of philosophy. He emphasized that the real poets are also creators; they create realities in the soul of the hearer or the reader. That was my spirit – I wanted to live my religious faith with my reason as well.

St. Paul wrote: "I will pray with the spirit and I will pray with the mind also; I will sing with the spirit and I will sing with the mind also . . . I would rather speak five words with the mind, in order to instruct others, than ten thousand words in a tongue" (1 Cor. 14 13-19). The problem is that I do not pray "in the spirit" as St. Paul did. With the prayer "in the spirit" the mind penetrates into the mystery and expresses the inexpressible aspects of the faith more clearly. This is the way the Fathers of the Church gave us doctrines, worship and spiritual life. They prayed "in the spirit" and they sang and taught with their mind "in the Holy Spirit." Without these two aspects of the faith highly developed, the Church loses in power and vitality. This is particularly true today, when the people are more sophisticated, thirsting for spirit and yet desiring knowledge also. For this reason many lose themselves in cultic mysticisms, which lead to extreme one-sidedness, or they become indifferent to the issues of faith.

My First Book

The lectures of Guardini fired my desire to learn more about Greek philosophy and more about human thought. I had not been initiated into the problem of the relationship of philosophy and Orthodox theology, and I was trying to grapple with it in an independent manner. My tendency is to understand the subjects of faith with clear thought as well. I do not mean to judge faith with reason. Faith is something that is given from above, a revelation from God. The mind can only have "a child's play" (παιδιάς) over the given issues of faith. Human reason is an "adorner" of the truth; it is not the creator of it. Human reason itself is a creation, a part of the one great truth. Only the Divine Logos is creative of all things (Jn. 1.3). When you walk in this manner, you do not fear lest you fall into heresy. This, I believe, is what the Holy Mountain offers: a grounding in the faith that nothing can shake. Many with only knowledge to guide them fall into heresy or even into unbelief, because they do not have a foundation in faith.

Every author judges the thought of others on the basis of his own thought. This is how I laid out the plan for my first book. I took the texts of Plato and of Aristotle – of "the Two," as I called them – as the basis of human thought. I then followed the six-volume work of Zeller as an initiation into Greek philosophy. My subject was Greek philosophy as a *propaedeia* – a preparation for Christianity. I do not mean for philosophy to show us what Christianity is, but rather for philosophy to show us that indeed human thought has need of Christ, is thirsting for Christ, for the truth, and that "the soul is by nature Christian." This is where Greek philosophy leads, to the thirst for something eternal, something real, something divine, which is to be found beneath and outside of our material world, which remains the source and the guarantee for the existence of this other world. And this other world was brought to us only by Christ. I concluded my book by writing that the philosophers brought us with a thirst to the source, to Christ. Now we have to bend down and drink from the source which has "living water . . . welling up to eternal life" (Jn. 4.10, 14; cf. 7.38).

America. Again, the Finger of God?

It is now 1950. I am working on my book. Metropolitan Michael of Corinth had become Archbishop of America. A friend of mine, a priest from our town, took the initiative without asking me to write about me to Archbishop Michael. Why? Only God knows.

In 1938, the chancellor of Corinth, Fr. Agathonikos, who later became Metropolitan of Argolidos first and then of Aigialeias and Kalavryta, had suggested that I go to America. For me he was "a true man to be a bishop." You could talk to him and he would listen to you as one human being to another. He had lived in America, and when he returned to Greece, Metropolitan Damaskenos had accepted him to be his chancellor. He showed me a dollar – something I had never seen before – and told me: "I'll get you the ticket and you will go to serve as a priest and teacher in America." I replied with conviction: "No, I prefer to go to Germany rather than America." The war had not yet started.

But now I have been to Germany and have received what I wanted, namely, the Greek philosophical manner of thinking. Metropolitan Michael is in America and he is inviting me to go there and assume the responsibility of the Community of St. Sophia in Los Angeles, California. "This must be the finger of God," I thought. "I shall go to America, learn English, and thus be able to work more effectively for my purpose." The invitation for America came during the McCarthy era. America then was fearful of every Communistic activity and would carry out austere investigations into the life of anyone who wanted to travel there, and especially those coming from Europe. A whole year passed and my papers had not been prepared. I went to Greece to see my family. I saw Fr. Agathonikos and he told me again to go to America. I simply said: "If the papers come soon."

Let me say parenthetically: Agathonikos had been to America. He had learned that I was being invited to America and had advised Archbishop Michael: "Do not bring Gerasimos to America." He wanted me now to stay in Greece.

My papers did not come. I stayed in Greece. I was appointed Spiritual Father to the student dormitory of *Apostoliki Diakonia*. This occurred in September of 1951, and I forgot about America. I decided to work in the Church of Greece. In March of 1952 I was visited by the young Bishop Athenagoras of Elaias, who later became Archbishop of Thyateira in Great Britain. "Archbishop Michael is again inviting you to go to America," he told me. "If you want, please write a letter to invite you officially." Was this another temptation or another finger of God? He invited me two times without my request. With my life in Greece, admittedly, I was not very satisfied. When someone leaves his place and lives in a different part of the world, his ideas change. Besides, my economic situation was not so good to help my sisters who had some need. Consequently, I accepted the invitation for Augusta, Georgia. Fr. Leonidas Contogiannis, a dynamic graduate of Holy Cross School of Theology, had been in the meantime appointed to Los Angeles. My papers had been prepared just in time, when the new law regarding military service had been in effect, whereby one could pay a sum of money instead of serving for two years. If the papers had been ready two months earlier, I would not have been allowed to travel abroad.

On July 3, 1952 I arrived in America. The news bulletins were announcing how many people would be killed during the holiday week-end of July 4 in all of America: 500-700 persons! It seemed to me like a great number of people, but in comparison with the total population this is not a greater percentage than those killed elsewhere.

At the Theological School of the Holy Cross

When I finally came to America Archbishop Michael decided to send me to the Theological School in Brookline Massachusetts. On July 8, Bishop Ezekiel, the Director of the School, came to meet me at the Archdiocese in New York and to escort me to the School. The trip from New York to Boston was most impressive. And even the ice cream treat: "the banana split" was too much for me. "This is America," they told me. And after that I was able to enjoy a banana split after my meals.

After four hours on the road we arrived at the Theological School in Brookline, a suburb of Boston. When we entered the campus of the School, I was amazed. The extensive fields of grass spotted with the yellow flowers of the dandelions, the many beautiful trees, the rhododendrons, the rose bushes – they were all so very beautiful to my sight. "It is good for us to be here," I said to myself. And so I remained and continue to remain in the School – longer than I have remained anywhere else in my life, and more than anyone else has remained in the School.

My appointment to the School was the best gift that I could ever ask from God. Back in 1942, on New Year's Eve, three *archimandrites* had declared what each one of us would pray for the new year. The two said: "To become a bishop." One became, the other to this day has not. I declared: "No. My wish is to become a professor, to teach." And God has granted me my wish. I thank Him and I glorify Him! Had I gone to Los Angeles, where I was first invited to go, I would have been lost, without English, among the rich and the powerful who directed the affairs of the Church. Even Fr. Contogiannis did not manage to do well there. He left to go to Oxford to do graduate studies. There I too would go later for a short stay.

Teaching

They appointed me professor and I was supposed to begin teaching in September. I did not know what I would be teaching so that I could prepare a little. At the University of Athens I did not have all the basic course because of the war. In Germany I studied a great deal, but primarily about the manner of thinking rather than systematic learning. The students had typewritten notes on the Letter to the Romans. I had a commentary in German. My strength was really the love for the students, who were being trained to become priests, co-workers in the salvation of souls, in this great country of America. I gathered whatever I had of faith and knowledge and gave my heart completely to their heart. I spoke from heart to heart, and not about theoretical teaching and learning. When we would come to questions with details, which did not have relevance for the essence of the faith, I would tell them: "What do you need such things for?" And in 1990, the Bishop of Boston repeated this question to me, thirty-eight years later!

What I wanted was to spur the interest, to think more deeply about the faith: Who is Christ? What has He brought that is new? Not merely in teaching but ontologically, in reality. When later the rockets were built that would be launched into space, which had explosions in three successive stages as they flew into outer space, I told the students: We have three explosions in the history of the world. The first is the creation, the second is the Incarnation of God for the salvation of the world in time (in the Church), and the third is our salvation in eternity. Later I learned that St. Gregory the Theologian used the expression of three explosions in the work of God.

I appreciate and enjoy the work of the critical researchers of the New Testament as far as it helps me to understand better that which I believe. Not to find out if this or that book was written by Paul or someone else. All the books of Sacred Scripture are the books of the believing Church. Critical research is not for finding out if Christ said something literally, but if Christ said something like that in his life; and it is about how John, the Beloved Disciple, understood it, lived it and transmitted it to us was the faith of the Church, "so that you too may believe." We are seeking for the faith of the Church, not the endless doubts and debates of the liberal theologians.

Am I a rationalist? Am I a Greek-speaking Protestant? Am

I a doubting Thomas? All of these labels have been applied to me. And perhaps I have a little of all of them. Even at the monastery someone had said to my Elder: "Your novice is going to become a heretic!" And this only because I wanted to examine everything. I cannot accept anything, unless I also understand somehow with my reasoning as well. However, when reason leaves more empty, then I surrender myself to Sacred Scripture: "It is so written . . . " I also say at every difficult subject. The issues of faith are difficult indeed even for the Fathers and for the Apostles.

Blessed are "the poor in spirit," the simple Christians who did not allow questions on the issues of faith. Such people live and experience the divine peace and serenity of the soul. However, the doubting Thomases and the questions existed in the past and will exist always, particularly in our days. It is difficult for one to have questions. And it is even more difficult to find someone to ask who will respect your questions (such as Bishop Demetrios of Vresthena and the professors of Oxford).

And if some of us who are responsible have some question, we can somehow give an answer with our faith and our thought, and in the final analysis with the "so it is written." But of course there are the questions of our faithful to which we must respond. If we do not respond, it may lead to indifference and disbelief.

Thirty-three years ago a young lady told me: "I have some questions." She had just finished college and was teaching catechism to our children. And now, in 1990, as she was going to teach, she called me and used the same phrase: "I have a question about Acts 20:26: '. . . that I am innocent of the blood of all of you . . .' "

N.E.F.O.S.

A young person connected me with the New England Federation of Orthodox Students. To this Federation of students Fr. Georges Florovsky would also speak on a regular basis. And this is how I got better acquainted with him. Gradually I began to communicate with our young people in English, always teaching and being taught in return from their ideas and their questions. The many questions about the Orthodox faith and life inspired me to ponder more deeply and with greater detail the matters of our faith, because it pleased me to be able to help the young people.

Faith and Life in Christ

"Blessed are they who have not seen and yet believed," that is, those who have believed without seeking logical proofs. And these are the people who have experienced the love of God in Christ, who have believed and who live their life in Christ with peace and serenity and spiritual joy. When we do not live according to the will of God, then it is difficult, impossible, to believe. The words of Christ are then not words of divine love, but of judgment against our works. Jesus said: "He who rejects me and does not receive my sayings has a judge; the word that I have spoken will be his judge on the last day" (Jn. 12.48). No one wants to hear that he is being judged, and he does not learn and does not believe (cf. Jn. 12. 37-48). Thus begin the questions and the doubts, not so much for the sake of learning, as to weaken the authority of Sacred Scripture, the voice of God, and to be spared the judgment. This is how the question is presented to Adam and Eve (Gen. 3.1-7).

On the contrary, "He who does the truth comes to the light ..." he knows where he is going, he believes and receives the power to become "a son of God," to be born of the Spirit of God from above (Jn. 1.12-13, 3.3, 17-21). Disbelief exists not because the things of faith are difficult. We all recognize that a way of life according to the Gospel would be the best both for each person and for all of society. But our difficulty lies in the fact that man who is free – and man is the only free being in the world – has a tendency toward evil, he "loves more the darkness rather than the light!" This is why someone said: "Man is not a problem that must be solved, but a mystery into which we must penetrate into order to understand it." This is the meaning of the classical: "Know thyself," which was taught by our ancient philosopher ancestors. Many of us, however, do not want to see ourselves in the mirror of our heart, because it is not so beautiful. We do not see the image of God in its purity residing inside us, as the Fathers of the Church tell us. St. Paul also says that we drink to get drunk so that we do not see our ugliness.

A Spirit of Contradiction

I was always a spirit of contradiction, as a clerk in my youth, in the monastery, and in our school. I have said that monks remain at the age of eighteen, but they think that they know everything. I could not understand why students who were 19-22 years old, had to study necessarily in the classroom and at designated times. Why couldn't they go out some sunny Sunday. Only on Thursday afternoon, until the time for supper, could they go off campus. There was no love, nor the mutual respect that is appropriate, between the Director and the professors of the School. The Director appointed me to be a responsible sub-Director, but he did not want me to tell him any of my opinions, nor would he even bother to ask me how I managed while he had been absent from the School for a week.

When he decided to reprimand me for neglecting the strict study hall rules to the point that the professors had to complain that our students were not studious, I could not control myself. This was my great weakness. I had to speak out and tell him directly how I saw the situation: "You are the cause of all this!" And I meant that there was no correct co-operation. This was harsh of me, but it just escaped. He then sought to have me removed from the School. He also stopped me from being sub-Director. This too was a blessing because it afforded me the time to complete my book, which still required a great deal of work.

The students, who knew that I had studied in Germany, and who wanted to show me some good will would daringly sing outside my window: "*Deutchland über Alles.*" I spoke with a friend who also had been hurt by the Director, and he answered: "That is how he is; you'll have to suffer the consequences." This was all very painful for me, because this otherwise good clergy brother did not have a single word of consolation to offer me. We all seemed to be working according to the letter of the law. Fortunately, I was always able to recognize my mistake. But I never regretted it because I believed that I was speaking the truth. Always I pray to God to give me patience and self control, because I know that with the gentle manner of love we can accomplish more and better things.

The Bishop Director appointed another sub-Director. But the students again showed their support by singing: "*Deutchland über Alles.*" I was then confined to teaching. This gave me the opportunity to prepare the final draft of my book and to have it published in 1954.

During this time the Archbishop wanted to bring a professor from Athens to be the Director of the School. A few months later the Archdiocese requested that the Bishop be confined to his pastoral duties for the Diocese and he took up residence for the first time in the new episcopal residence at 170 Pond Street, Jamaica Plain, a nearby section of Boston.

The Archbishop requested from the University of Athens to send him a professor who could serve as Director of the School. Because this did not happen, Archimandrite Nicon Patrinacos was appointed to be the Director of the School. I remained as a professor. I came to love the students and they in turn loved me, and with this love I remained in the School for ten years, which were the very best years of my life. Certain students, who tended to make comments about their professors, gave me the pseudonym *ΓΚΑΠ*: "Gerasimos, understanding, love, faith." The first yearbook of the School, published in 1958, was dedicated to me.

My Election as a Bishop

For Christmas Eve, 1961, I had been invited to serve at Sts. Constantine and Helen Church in Brooklyn, New York. I visited Archbishop Iakovos, who, among other things, told me this: "We need to get better organized and I have submitted your name as a candidate for bishop in Detroit." There was not as yet a diocese in Detroit. I gave no answer at that moment. All night I thought about the change that would take place in my life. I loved to teach so much, and each year I was becoming all the more confident in my work. I did not see myself having any administrative capabilities. Thus, the day after Christmas I asked him to recall his proposal for my election. He then asked me if I had any preference between Detroit and Charlotte, North Carolina. But if it meant that I had to leave the School, it didn't really matter where I would go. In a few days he called me and told me: "Since you so love the

School, I have decided to keep you in Boston. You will assume responsibilities on July 1, 1962." In the meantime he had also decided to transfer Bishop Meletios to Chicago. My ordination took place at the Cathedral of Boston on May 20, 1962 by Archbishop Iakovos with Bishop Meletios of Christianopoulis and Bishop Timothy of Rodostolon as co-celebrants.

As Bishop

"If any one aspires to the office of bishop, he desires a noble task" (1 Tim. 3.1). The office of bishop is indeed sacred, but the responsibilities are very difficult. The bishop himself is not perfect, nor is the flock perfect. And the bishop will often come into conflict with persons, with priests, with the organized community. I followed the middle way. I listened and accepted the opinion of everyone, and made the best possible judgment. In matters of faith I applied the rule of strict interpretation. In matters of secondary importance *economia* or flexibility was applied, in order to avoid unnecessary conflicts. I served for fifteen years and did not come into serious conflict with anyone. Neither did I have any great achievements. However, the programs of community life functioned well, according to the capabilities of the priests. In Boston itself I encountered greater difficulties. I was inexperienced and the people, it seemed to me, were perhaps more demanding and difficult. And with the people, the priests were also more difficult. The people in the Pittsburgh area and Diocese seemed to me to be simpler, more hospitable to the bishop. However, nowhere did I encounter any insoluble problems.

Co-operation with the Priests

I always had close co-operation with the priests. I always

welcomed their opinions and ideas. I wanted them to know their position and their responsibility in the Church. They were my officers and my soldiers. I used to tell them that they were the bishops in their communities for 364 days of the year. I could communicate with their faithful only once a year. They knew better than I the joys and the problems of their faithful and they could organize and carry out the spiritual programs with the encouragement and co-operation of the bishop. The best communication I had with the priests was during the general clergy gatherings, and particularly the weekly ones in various regions of the Diocese of Pittsburgh. We exchanged our thoughts freely on all the issues and problems we faced. We enjoyed lunch together and parted in peace. Without this regular communication with his priests the bishop feels isolated and alone in his office. When the Archbishop recommended a transfer to Charlotte for a warmer climate, I feared the absence of the priests and I asked him not to transfer me. Thus, I remained in Pittsburgh until my retirement.

The Bishop and the Archbishop

I undertook my responsibilities as bishop with the hope of a close co-operation with the Archbishop. I knew his capabilities and I awaited for personal co-operation, direction and assistance. I did not have it as much as I had dreamed of it. Perhaps he took my capability for granted and did not wish to appear to be meddling in my ministry. In general, however, all the bishops would receive directions and ideas about our ministry from him. Sometimes there were differences of opinion, and no one could be absolutely certain of his opinion on any one issue. We always attempted, with a spirit of love, to solve the problems for the good of the Church.

The Problem of Inter-Faith Marriages

In our country inter-faith marriages between Orthodox Christians and non-Orthodox Christians are increasing greatly. And the Church has accommodated these in a pastoral manner, without too many insurmountable difficulties. However, a far more complex and difficult problem is the marriage of an Orthodox Christian with a non-Christian and particularly a Jew. The Canons do not permit such a marriage. Today, however, we are confronted by a very particular reality. Our young men and women establish close relationships with young Jewish men or women with serious intentions.

The question arises: Are we going to condemn the Orthodox spouse? Are we going to cut him or her off completely from Christ? Or can we, by the application of dispensation and economy, bless such a marriage for the sake of the Orthodox spouse? We would, of course, not encourage such marriages, since, under any circumstance, they present very difficult problems in their family life. Faith is an essential element in the life of the family. However, once there is a serious relationship between an Orthodox Christian and a Jewish person, and the Orthodox member desires to remain a Christian, what are we to do? Are we going to recommend a divorce? This is a harsh and cruel measure. Are we going to cut off a believer from Christ because a life has joined with that of a Jewish person? This is an even harsher and crueler measure. Who can separate such a person from the love of Christ? In a conversation with bishops, a metropolitan of the Ecumenical Patriarchate said that in Turkey they sometimes, out of necessity, permit the marriage of a Greek Orthodox with a Muslim Turk. Then I proposed that we discuss the subject of Jewish spouses, but the appropriate authorities did not agree. And yet this issue must become the subject of serious discussion in the Church. In fact, today when we are seeking contacts and dialogues with all the religions, we have no right to cut off a believer from Christ, only because he or she loves some non-Christian and they have decided to marry. We lose our children completely this way. Would St. Paul have done it?

Worship Services Can Be Abbreviated

Once the Archbishop asked us in a letter to think about the abbreviation of the Divine Liturgy. The issue is very sensitive. However, the question was posed, therefore, the problem exists. My answer was this: "I believe that the Liturgy can be shortened, or rather simplified a little. Cut out some of the repetitions, without omitting anything from the inspired and magnificent prayers. Before this is done, however, we should study the subject in its essential nature. We must not simply refer to the Typikon." As an example, I referred to the Liturgy of St. John Chrysostom, which is briefer, without being in any way inferior to that of St. Basil. And certainly no one was scandalized then by this abbreviation. Now, the Liturgy of the Presanctified Gifts was incorporated, in a way, into the Service of Vespers, without losing any of its magnificence and contrite spirit. Everything is a matter of conditioning, except of course the essential doctrines of the faith, the sacrifice and our participation in salvation. Instead of two entrances in the Liturgy we could have only the one. The meaning of the entrances is no longer meaningful as in the past. The same may be said of those repetitions: "Let us again..." and "Peace be with you..." etc. The prayers can be recited in a low voice, while the faithful congregation, knowing what is going on at that time, will pray with their heart, with their own words. How such things can be decided and how they can be implemented is an issue of serious study by the whole Church.

The Main Aspect of My Work

The main aspect of my work was pastoral, both toward the people as well as toward the priests in particular. It was to the priests that I always entrusted the activities of our communities. I would assist those who somehow were limited and hold back those who tended to be too liberal. They were my officers. Always in my sermons, lectures, and conversations I would emphasize the sacredness of the faith in the person of Christ and in the life and mission of the Church, and particularly of Orthodoxy. I would say that Orthodoxy is like a small shop with very select merchandise next to the large market place of the other multitudinous ecclesiastical communities, or even of the world as a whole. We cannot compete with them in numbers. Our responsibility is to demonstrate to all the particular spirituality that characterizes the Orthodox Faith and way of life. But we can only demonstrate this when we live Orthodoxy in an Orthodox way. It cannot be done with a scholastic understanding of the doctrines, which even our professional theologians have difficulties in expressing to the people in a simple and understandable manner. The beauty of Orthodoxy is her profound faith in Christ as the Apostles knew Him and loved Him, and as the great Fathers of the One, Holy, Catholic and Apostolic Church have presented Him to us in the depth of the prayers, the services, and above all in the spiritual masterpiece of the Divine Liturgy. Our Liturgy is not simply the work of one or two of the Fathers, such as Basil the Great and John Chrysostom. The Liturgy is the life experience and the expression of the living faith of the whole Church throughout the ages. One who does not understand and does not live and experience what is going on during the Divine Liturgy is not yet an Orthodox Christian. Such a person does not experience the reality of Christ, of the Church, in all of His depth and height.

I made mistakes in my difficult task. Certainly I did not offer as much as a bishop should, living in twentieth century America. I hope the Lord will judge me according to the measure of my weaknesses, according to my "two talents," and will say to me: "Well done good and faithful servant!" (Mt. 25.23). But this only God can say.

The Greek Language

The main problem facing the Archdiocese of America is the language problem. When I came to America I was not conscious of a need for the English language. At the School everything was done in Greek. The students spoke in Greek. This of course helped them to learn the Greek language very well, which was necessary in our Church, because of her composition. On July 15, 1952, Bishop Ezekiel, two students and I went to Pittsburgh for the Choir Convention of the area. There were about 300 young people gathered there for a wonderful program. I observed to my surprise that virtually no one there was speaking in Greek! And in 1952 the grandmothers who had come from Greece were still speaking some Greek at home for the children and grandchildren to hear. Nevertheless, they conversed among themselves only in English. I could not understand them and felt like an outsider. From this convention I was taught that the language of our young people, under 40 years of age, is only English. Naive as always, I wrote down my thoughts on this subject. Religion is not a matter of language; it is a matter of faith . . . I sent this article to the Archdiocese and it was published in the "Orthodox Observer," the official publication of the Archdiocese. No one among the administrators or the professors of the School spoke to me personally, but I learned that they had criticized me for hastily writing about the situation in America before I even had the opportunity to become familiar with it.

In 1956 I proposed that our students should be trained in giving sermons in English. In a conversation, my friend and colleague, Fr. Silas told me: "No English yet! Maybe after ten years." But for our priests to preach in English after ten years, they must begin to learn now. In any case, the English sermon was soon introduced into the academic program of the School. In 1964 the Clergy-Laity Congress in Denver decided that the Epistle, the Gospel, the Creed and the Lord's Prayer could also be recited in English.

In 1970 at the Clergy-Laity Congress in New York we recognized officially that it is necessary to introduce more English, particularly in parishes where there are many interfaith marriages, where many young people do not understand Greek and cannot worship with us. The Greek newspapers at the time made a big issue of this decision, and the Archbishop was obliged to send an Encyclical directing the priests to use only as much English as was permitted by the Denver Congress in 1964. At the time I wrote: "No more English than you already have up to now." After the Congress I traveled from Maine to Colorado and then to California. Everyone that I talked with seriously agreed that if we have half-Greek and half-English, it would be all right. People have been alarmed that Greek might be excluded altogether. We need to be better informed and enlightened.

The issue of language troubled me a great deal. Language is not only a problem; it is also a tragedy. We cannot abandon the Greek language, nor can we ignore the need for English. In an interview that I gave in Pittsburgh for the periodical of the Cathedral there in 1977, I noted that 25% of Greek should always remain in the Greek Orthodox Church in America.

The reason for this is the fact that Greek is the original language of Sacred Scripture and of worship, and because constantly new immigrants are coming from Greece. To want to keep everything in Greek in the Liturgy is like wanting the faithful and the people around us not to be able to understand us. It is as if we want the Church to be only for the senior members and for the immigrants from Greece.

This is why I considered it my duty to write to our Patriarch and to plead with him to speak up about the language issue:

To His All Holiness Athenagoras
The Ecumenical Patriarch

October 15, 1970

Your All Holiness,

Please accept what follows most respectfully as the actual confession of a son to a father.

For eighteen years I have been serving the Greek Orthodox Church of Christ in America. At the suggestion of His Eminence our Archbishop, Your paternal love elevated me to the office of bishop. A noble task but difficult. For this reason I always avoided it. Duty bound I study the needs of the present and attempt to foresee the future of the Church in this country of dramatic progress in all the directions of life.

Your All Holiness knows through personal contacts the development of our Church during the last twenty years. The Clergy-Laity Congress has demonstrated that the composition of the members of the Church has been reversed. The representatives of our Communities, now ninety percent American born, see their church as a Church in America, destined to serve their children who are Americans of Greek descent, with only the English language and with the certainty that only fifty percent of them will be married with young men or women of Greek descent.

Worship in the Greek language does not hold for them the attraction it once had for the first generation children of the immigrants. They want to hear English, to pray in English, and to realize that they are well informed and conscientious Orthodox Christians.

Last year when the two hour Christmas Service ended, the choir sang "Silent Night." The choir director with relief told the priest: "Father, now I realized that we are celebrating Christmas!" This means that the entire service had been done merely mechanically. It gave them nothing like a message of Christmas. How harsh and sad this is!

Many spouses among those who have inter-faith marriages would probably choose to espouse sincerely the Orthodox Faith. Many other Christians as well are seeking to approach our Church. Yet, with only the Greek language they cannot understand her spiritual life in all of its grandeur. They see only symbolic gestures, which remain mere symbols "sealed by seven seals" that cannot touch the depth of the soul.

This type of worship satisfies only a few persons. Certain people do rise up to defend the Greek language. Not because they know well the content of worship in Greek, but simply because they want to be considered heroes, perhaps so that "they may not be persecuted for the sake of the cross of Christ."

It is true of course that prudence and vigilance is needed in charting the direction we travel. Yet, the voice must be heard: Our Church is not only for the truly admirable Greek pioneers or for those who even now come from Greece. The Church is for our American-born children and grandchildren, for all of America, if not for all the world.

If English is not introduced soon in good measure into our worship, our Church shall remain for the majority of our children and our friends in America a lifeless formality, worthy of some sympathy, but never a serious expression of Christian faith that renews lives. Our Church will thus not be worthy of the attention and the respect she deserves. Nor will our Church be able to assume her proper place in the spiritual life of this country.

The responsibility is great. No escapism is justifiable. The voice of the leaders must be direct, clear and sincere in defense of the truth. This truth, which I know from experience, is accepted by ninety-nine percent of those who are complaining today. But they are complaining because they fear the complete abolishment of the Greek language. And they are seeking to find out the truth in all of its breadth and depth, in faith and in love, in grace and in truth. They want to hear that the English being introduced is not meant to dishonor the Greek language, but rather to help our children hold on to the living and immortal Greek spirit, as expressed in the Orthodox Christian Faith and worship.

Your All Holiness, please accept the supplication of one of your spiritual sons. You have done so much for the Church. Your work, however, will remain incomplete if you do not give the appropriate attention to the missionary Church of America. Raise your Patriarchal voice in defense of our Church in America. It is the only voice that can and must be heard with the appropriate attention, so that it may bring about the fruit of love, of peace, the fruit of the Spirit, for which you have sacrificed your entire life.

Beseeching your blessings upon these matters, I conclude...

The issue of language is indeed a dramatic one for our Church. The priests must know the Greek language well, and Greek should be taught in all of the theological schools. However, the work of the Church will have to be done in English, and the priests must know it well to compete with the other theologians and preachers in this country.

There are many conversations going on about the teaching of Greek, but we need to study the matter together, according to the capabilities we have, and to find the best possible solutions. The first school must, of course, be the home.

Today a sufficient amount of English has been introduced into the Divine Liturgy. This is particularly true in certain cities where English-speaking Greeks and inter-faith marriages are in the majority. A short sermonette of three minutes is needed to give epigrammatically and clearly the message of the Gospel. After this it is necessary to develop the message more fully in English for all. All the Greeks speak English because they live among the Americans.

At Oxford

After I had served three years as a bishop, I requested a leave of absence to go to England. I was asked: "Why, what will you do there?" "To talk, to discuss theological issues," I replied. "But there they talk, and you are not known for talking a lot," the Archbishop told me. "With whom should I talk?" I replied, and that ended our exchange.

After a conversation over some difficult problems, Fr. Alchin asked me: "What do you expect to learn from the professors?" I replied: "I'll hear something, at least I'll confirm my thoughts." I was free. I had no responsibilities, no telephone calls. Like a young student I walked around the colleges of Oxford University to hear, to discuss. I had lost the opportunity to sit sufficiently at the desk of the University in Athens because of the war. We sat with some eleven professors in all for an hour, an hour and a half, discussing one on one issues of common concern.

I recall discussing the mission of Christ in the book of Hebrews (Heb. 10.5f). We talked about the Logos, about the ontologically new element that Christ brought into the world. We talked about life after death, and many other similar subjects. From each professor I was able to receive something. My soul was being satisfied. This is what I had wanted. I am an egoist; I wanted to satisfy myself, my mind, my heart.

I was planning to meet three more professors in Glasgow and Edinburgh when I received a telegram requiring my immediate return to the United States. "I received what I wanted," I thought to myself. Had I stayed any more it would have been primarily for the English language. The telegraph was from God at the appropriate hour. I returned to assume the administration of the Theological School because certain problems had appeared.

My Resignation from the Administrative Duties of Being a Bishop

Administrative duties always wearied me. It is not possible to easily compromise justice and love. Only God could do that and He did it in Christ. When Fr. Harakas asked me how I felt about being Director of the School, I said that it seems like "to administer is to sin." I always wanted to resign, to find peace, to study, and perhaps to write. However, the responsibilities of being a bishop did not leave me the necessary time.

On September 9, 1975 the Archbishop asked me if I wanted

to assume the responsibility of director and organizer of the Spiritual Center at the Academy of St. Basil. I would serve as the spiritual father to the priests, and make the center a clinic of the soul. I answered him on the next day by conveying to him my thoughts on the project. He did not answer me. I realized however that he would not mind if I resigned from my episcopal duties. Thus, on December 17, 1976 I declared my desire to be relieved of my pastoral responsibilities as of July 31. On December 21 His Eminence accepted my request. This acceptance seemed to me a message that even in my resignation the hand of God was present.

Thus, on July 31, 1977, my administrative responsibilities as a bishop ended. From spiritual responsibilities a clergyman and every spiritual person is never relieved. He is always seeking for something more, something better. He never accomplishes enough in this life. The struggle continues with the failures and the successes until the Lord calls him.

Farewell Banquet: June 19, 1977

We celebrated the Divine Liturgy at the cathedral church of St. Nicholas in Pittsburgh with His Eminence, our Archbishop, officiating. That evening we had the farewell banquet. It had been well-organized by my friend Dino Christakis. With photographs which apparently had been secretly gathered from my office, they presented my life in a slide presentation. This was very emotional for me. A life in pictures that spanned from 15 to 67 years before my eyes, alive. That evening was a sacred experience for me. I was celebrating the end of my service, the end of my active life – so there is an end to life? On such occasions one can actually believe it – that there is an end for all things in this life! And it is only the hope of Christian faith that gives real meaning to human life. On such occasions faith in Christ and in eternity is tested and strengthened. I had similar experiences, at the death of my mother, and that of Archbishop Damaskenos of Athens. I thought to myself, that if the life of such people simply ends in death, then life surely has no meaning. Without the Resurrection, we Christians would surely be the most miserable of all people (1 Cor. 15.19-20).

On June 17, 1935 I had been ordained Deacon by Metropolitan Damaskenos of Corinth. On June 19, 1977 I concluded my active service – forty-two years of service, a multi-faceted service to the Church. I grew up as a young shepherd, near the sheep and with my father, the good shepherd. I concluded my work as a shepherd of people. May the Lord judge my work according to "His great mercy" and not according to exacting justice.

I tried not to show my emotion. But the pain of being separated from so many people that I loved and who loved me was truly great. When in 1967 I left Boston for Pittsburgh it was a painful experience. When I entered the Pennsylvania Turnpike and looked around me, I thought to myself: "Gerasime, these people here are now your flock and these you must now love." And I did love them and they loved me. And here precisely lies the whole essence and the meaning of life – in the love which does not end in this life nor in the other life, because God Himself is love. (My friend, Bob Bethony, once called me traitor when he did not want me to leave Boston). The canons of the Church are just in not wanting the bishop to be transferred or to abandon his flock – "the children that God has given me." We are human, however, and sometimes, for the good of the Church, even the law has to be put aside. I have everyone in my prayers and I want their prayers and their love.

I had asked that we should not have present at the banquet people outside of our Church communities. I wanted to be alone with my flock, my spiritual children. I wanted to confess to them freely, to speak to them about their short-comings, to congratulate them for their achievements and their love. And above all, I wanted to speak to them about their future, the future of the Orthodox Church in this blessed country of America in the western hemisphere. Those of us who came from Greece held our faith high during our first steps. The newer generations now must present the Ortho-dox faith and life to a world that is thirsting for it. They must give the faith in a living and radiant manner, as it really is, as we have received it.

I thanked everyone from my heart, and I thanked and con-tinue to thank God for His love and His mercy in my life. May God bless our Church.

Return to Our School

At the beginning of August 1977 I departed for Greece. I visited many places. I went to the Holy Mountain, to my roots. The monastery of my repentance was in ruins. I do not know what I would have done if were not in ruins. I went to Kefallonia, to the Church of St. Gerasimos. I venerated the Saint for the first time. I also went to Trikala of Corinth and visited the house where he had grown up.

I had not yet decided: Should I remain in Greece or return to America? In America I lived the major portion of my life, of my career. The most beautiful part of my life in America was at the Theological School. Thus, after verbal invitations, I wrote to the Archbishop: "I shall come to America only to be at the Theological School, and only if I am invited without reservations. I do not want to go as a bishop, nor to interfere in its sacred mission." Dr. Lelon invited me immediately by overnight letter. Thus, in November, 1977, I found myself again at our Theological School, embraced by the love of all. There I find myself, reading, teaching occasionally, writing and praying.

What pleased me very much at the School was the opportunity to teach again for several years, to communicate with the students. I taught dogmatics for the first time. There I was able to see the thinking of the Fathers of our Church. The basis of their thought was the personal experience of salvation in Christ, as lived and transmitted to us by the Apostles; as lived by the Fathers of the Church in their daily life with prayer, study and teaching. And above all, as they lived it in their sacramental life – as partakers of the Body and the Blood of Christ, as partakers of divine nature, of theosis . . .

At the School I had the opportunity to write my book: *Orthodoxy – Faith and Life: Christ in the Gospels and in the Church*. I wanted to dedicate this book at the end of my service as an expression of gratitude, first to God, and then to the faithful who loved me and strengthened me in my work. This is my life of eighty years – the higher limit acknowledged by David. After all this time, I still see that human life is and remains a mystery. And we must penetrate into ourselves, if we are to understand it as a mystery in the hands of God, "For from him and through him and to him are all things. To him be glory for ever. Amen" (Rom. 11.36).

Gerasimos Papadopoulos:
The Bishop of Love and Peace

Ambrose-Aristotle Zographos

Having found mercy from God, I too was fortunate to be numbered among the great multitude of spiritual children of the ever memorable Spiritual Father, His Grace Bishop Gerasimos of Abydos.

The attempt to sketch the illumined person and the many-faceted personality of the Elder–*Geronta* is a difficult undertaking, destined for other charismatic biographers. This is why what follows is nothing more than some humble brush-strokes based on personal recollections or remarks that I have heard from others who lived close to him.

When the Elder fell asleep in the Lord, the experience of spiritual orphanage inaugurated in me a barrage of recollections from his holy life, and my attempt to record them served as a redemptive salve in moments of profound pain and grief. I offer these recollections as one insignificant *antidoron* for all that he has done to support me spiritually and morally, and with the hope that they shall contribute to the spiritual benefit of those who shall read them.

***

In the academic year 1981-2, Stylianos Papadopoulos, the beloved nephew of the Elder and my highly respected professor of Patrology at the University of Athens, was explaining to us who in truth is a "Father and Teacher of the Church." My mind traveled to other distant times and in my youthful imagination, I attempted to comprehend the person and the characteristics of the "Father and Teacher of the Church." Never did I imagine that when I came to America I would find a contemporary Father of the Church in the person of His Grace Bishop Gerasimos of Abydos, our most beloved and much-mourned Elder.

When I first met the holy Elder, my soul was at peace with him. His holy life transfused in me, through word and silence, something of the divine Love, and his serene fatherly image reminded me of the saintly image of the patron of my birthplace, St. Nectarios.

During those blessed and unforgettable hours of the Mystery of Confession when I confided the burden of my sins upon his sacred stole, I would find in the person of the Elder a wise guide and a prototype of the good shepherd. Through his prudent, well grounded, and God-inspired advice, the outpouring of his experience acquired through ascetic effort on Mt. Athos and through his long and productive service in the Church, I was experiencing a foretaste of the joy and sweetness of paradise.

He never offered me many or lofty words about prayer. But he taught me, and the entire academic community of Holy Cross School of Theology, the unceasing prayer of the heart with his life which radiated prayer. With his daily routine, he taught us, as St. Makarios of Egypt taught his students, that during the time of prayer, "There is no need for unnecessary talk. Stretch out your arms and say: 'Lord, have mercy as you know.' If war is imminent, say: 'Lord, help!' And He knows what is for our benefit and will provide mercy for us" (PG.

65.269). As a monk who loved the liturgical services, Bishop Gerasimos would come daily to his beloved chapel of the Holy Cross – unhindered by the weight of years, illness or unfavorable climatic conditions. Thus, he taught us with his own asceticism never to abandon the work of prayer which is loved by God, never to find excuses "in our sinfulness." We would see him each morning and evening in the chapel, often with raised hands, praying in his particular corner – that corner of the chapel which now, too, is orphaned. Now, as we enter the chapel, we turn our glance toward his empty corner, trying intently to hear the voice of his supplication, which he would raise to the God of Love. The "Lord have mercy," and the "Glory to You, O Lord, glory to You," which were often heard aloud from his blessed lips as an outpouring of his heart during the sacred services – but not only this – shall be for all of us a powerful lesson of prayer. This was a lesson that all of us students – Greek-speaking and English-speaking – could readily understand. And this was so because no one ever stopped to think if your prayer – beloved Elder – was uttered in Greek or in English. We are grateful to you because you taught us with your life to pray, not with human languages, but with the mystical and experiential language of the heart.

The unforgettable holy Elder was and shall always be a precious gift not only for the Holy Cross School of Theology, but also for the whole Orthodox Church in America. By his virtuous life he made palpable and perceptible the presence of holiness in our own time. We glorify God and are grateful to our Elder because "the saint is [not] absent" and "the faithful have [not] vanished" (Ps. 12.1) from our materialistic society.

Moreover, his authentic ecclesiastical prudence was expressed in his initial refusal to accept the responsibility of a bishop, his later obedience to the voice of the Church, and, finally, his premature retirement from the active episcopacy. He often said, "There were others better than I." This is the best lesson of a true ecclesiastical ethos for those ambitious persons who "desire to be bishops" without considering the cost and the responsibility of such awesome service. I shall never forget something he confided in me when he was speaking about the tremendous responsibility he felt as a Hierarch: "My son, I never ascended the episcopal throne with ease. How can I tell you – I never felt comfortable in high places because I was not worthy. I'm not saying this out of a sense of humility; it was the truth!"

The list of virtues which in Christ adorned the wholeness of the personality of our ever-memorable Elder is indeed long and difficult to record in detail. For this reason an attempt will be made to refer, ever so briefly, to the most characteristic of his virtues.

Above all the Elder was adorned with the crown jewel of the virtues – love. "Love, love" he would repeat in his sermons, his lectures and in his private conversations. "My son, I can understand all the sins," he told me once during a confession, "but the absence of love, which goes as far as to not be able to say 'Good morning' to someone, and the lie which makes us children of Satan, the father of lies, this I cannot understand. It is impossible for me. This is why I am very strict in confession with sins which injure love and truth."

The following incidents are also characteristic of the convictions of the Elder regarding the subject of Christian love.

Three students were talking with the Elder once. Suddenly a hornet appeared among them, and one of the frightened students attempted to scare it away. "No, my son," the Elder told him, "don't do that. Become a friend to your enemies and you'll never have enemies."

One day another student told him: "Your Grace, I cannot understand the Lord's word about forgiving someone 'seventy times seven'. There are unscrupulous people who take advantage of it. They consider us stupid. How many times can we allow them to make fools of us?"

"My son, Christ said that we must never grow weary in forgiving. Have you truly considered how many times He may have proven to have been a fool himself?" That was the wise but also disarming response of the Elder.

Once, after following a lengthy discussion of many hours with representatives of the ecumenical movement, I accompanied the Elder to his cell. On the way he told me: "Everything that we discussed today was without meaning. The union of the churches is not going to come about with theological loquacity. What we need, my son, is love, love and prayer." Then he told me the following story: "When I was bishop of Boston, a group of zealous anti-ecumenists came to my office and tried to trick me in conversation, as the Pharisees attempted with our Lord. So, rather slyly, they asked me: 'Your Grace, what is your opinion about the pope?' 'Let me tell you, my friends,' I replied. 'Personally I feel guilty because I am not praying for the pope as much as I should.' The zealots lowered their faces and departed in shame and, hopefully, with their lesson learned," concluded the Elder.

When the Elder listened to theologians with a cultural bent of mind discussing sublime and incomprehensible theories, he recoiled spontaneously and often reminded them of the faith and the love for God and man which simple people like his parents had.

"During World War II my mother was profoundly troubled, seeing human blood spilled with so much thoughtless detachment and unscrupulousness. Once, when I went down to the village, she asked me: 'Will we ever find mercy from God for killing our fellow human beings and our brothers? What does it matter if they are Germans or Italians? I hate the war!' I assure you," the Elder admitted to me, "that I, the theologian, had never thought about that which had so profoundly moved my uneducated mother who spoke as a true theologian!"

Peace was the second main characteristic of the Elder that distinguished his personality. His love for peace was impressed upon his serene face. We would look upon him and he would transmit to us a heavenly peacefulness. A priest, a former student at Holy Cross, told me a few days after the falling asleep in the Lord of the Elder: "When I would look upon him, I felt such serenity and peace in my soul that I did not need anything else. This is why I would not go to speak privately with him. Why should I disturb him, I thought, since I received what I needed by simply looking upon him?"

It is certainly not fortuitous that, as far as I know, the first miracle of the Elder, after his saintly falling asleep in the Lord, was the peace and the love he brought to the hearts of two clergymen who had been at odds with each other for a long time before. The Elder had been observing their coldness and often remarked: "I am very troubled by such things, my son. I do not want to hear and believe that such problems exist between fellow clergy. We must pray for this situation." And his prayer was heard. The miracle apparently took place during the funeral service of the Elder, where both of these clergymen were present. The dove of peace and love returned and rested upon their hearts.

The Elder was unabatedly and faithfully dedicated throughout his entire life to the diptych of Love-Peace. Wherever he was he would underscore with his life the eternal value of the love of God, and would contribute in every way possible for peace to prevail among men. Thus, now that his holy soul is eternally at peace near the God of Love and Peace, it can be said that to him deservedly belongs the title of "Bishop of Love and Peace."

Besides the unfeigned love and peace, however, a significant place in the soul of the Elder was taken up by his humble spirit and unaffected simplicity, which serve as the surest way to the Kingdom of Heaven. He practiced the patristic code of "living without notice" (λάθε βιώσας), and this is why he lived in obscurity, avoiding any disturbance or "getting entangled at the feet" of anyone, as he would say in his characteristic manner. He knew how to carefully conceal his charisms and his virtues that he may not lose them. Such was his simplicity and his humility that if you saw him without knowing who he was, it was very difficult to understand that he was, for example, a bishop, or that he possessed an extensive education. In this respect the contribution of the Elder to the prospective clergymen in the School of Theology was of tremendous value, given the fact that, unfortunately, the fragrant flowers of humility and simplicity do not always fare well in ecclesiastical and theological environments. Moreover, the humble and simple form of life of the Elder was and will be an excellent response to the "Orthodox presbyterians" who may in a timely or untimely fashion attack the episcopal office, on account of the behavior of certain higher clergymen, who, as St. Isidore of Pelusium said, "do not administer worthily as good stewards but appropriate dishonestly as rulers" (PG 78.1337). And this is because the Elder was never "a ruling bishop," but a humble ascetic Bishop in whose presence anyone could be at ease and have a great sense of freedom of movement.

During the Divine Liturgy, if a deacon or anyone else attempted to serve the Elder by helping him to put on his vestments, he would often say, "Please, leave me to vest myself; you go and do your work."

All of us would see the Elder wearing a simple cassock and a monastic *skoufos* and walking humbly, simply, and quietly around the campus of the School of Theology. He lived in a humble cell like one of the students. He was frugal and ascetic in all of his ways, never having forgotten his monastic identity. The high offices never robbed him of his spiritual treasure. This attitude was obvious in his manner regarding food. He observed strictly the commandment of the Lord to His disciples: "Eat whatever is set before you . . . " (1 Cor. 10.27). We never heard our respected Elder complain about the food. He would go down to the cafeteria of the School, bless the food if some other clergyman had not already blessed it, take his tray and sit at a table with students. If someone offered, out of respect, to bring him something or to take his tray away at the end of the meal, he rarely ever accepted to be served. He accepted only when our persistence caused him to yield, or when he would perceive that his refusal would wound some overly sensitive soul.

"*Geronta*, allow me to drive you up to your cell with my car so you won't get tired walking." "It is better that I walk; it does me good," would be his usual response. I often had the exceptional blessing and honor to drive him to his endeared friends, Mr. Demetrios and Mrs. Dionysia Yphantis. I realized how comfortable he felt in the company of these hospitable people of love, who had helped and offered hospitality to so many students, professors, and visitors to the School. In the end the Elder never omitted to express his gratitude and his sincere thank you for the hospitality. He was always deeply impressed by the customary response Mr. Yphantis made to expressions of thanksgiving: "Your Grace, do not say, 'Thank you.' It does not cost anything to be good!"

Permit me, finally, to mention ever so briefly three more basic points, which constituted the beautiful Byzantine mosaic of the holy personality of the Elder, and thus to conclude my remarks. Otherwise, I would be in danger of succumbing to the temptation of loquaciousness, which is most inappropriate and utterly contrary to the measured and discreet spirit of the Elder.

First, I mention the spirit of thirst for learning which distinguished him always. This is the reason we would see him listening with great interest to the lectures of a young student, or to the homilies and sermons in the chapel (even those given by students as part of their training in the course of Homiletics), and studying without interruption, never losing an opportunity for learning.

"Do not presume that we Orthodox know everything. We have much to learn from the heterodox. If you are a humble student, you will become even more Orthodox over there . . . " he would say to me when, with his blessing, I went to study at Princeton.

Once when I asked him on the telephone what he was doing, he replied: "I am reading again and learning John the Evangelist. I thought I knew him. But now I realize that I knew nothing, even though I had studied him and had taught him to my students so many times."

Second, his love for nature revealed his own soul's inner beauty. As an authentic friend of God, the Elder could not help but be attracted to the beauty of the creation of God. All of us who knew him well remember him with the pruning hook and the watering can in hand caring with delight for the flowers, the plants, and the trees. He would be deeply hurt, like the Fathers of the desert, whenever he would see profane human hands destroying nature! The following incident is most characteristic of him. One day a group of students were playing soccer just beyond the little flower garden of the Elder. He was watching them from his window, and each time the ball would go into his rose bushes, his sensitive heart would be pained, would bleed. In the afternoon at Vespers he said the following:

"My dear students, tonight I must tell you that at first I felt pain each time the ball was kicked into the flowers. Then I became angry. I got really angry. And as I was preparing to go down and scold the students who were playing soccer, I stopped and spoke first to God. I asked him what I should do. And He told me: 'Let it go, they are children and they want to play.' With that my soul became calm again . . . and you were spared a serious punishment!"

I remember how, whenever we would drive by the gracious building overlooking Jamaica Pond where the old Diocese of Boston was housed, the Elder would ask me to stop so that he might look over and admire the various blooming trees which he himself had planted years before as Bishop of Boston. He would admire the flowers, give glory to God and bless himself, saying the verses from the Psalm: "O Lord, how manifold are thy works! In wisdom has thou made them all" (Ps. 104.24). I stood there speechless in his presence as he rejoiced as a little child observing the work of his hands in bloom. In this way he taught me to love nature and to appreciate the miracles of the creation of God.

And, finally, a word about the sense of humor of the Elder. Spontaneous and natural humor is characteristic of the Saint. The Saints, restored by the grace of God, preserve the integrity of the human person before the fall, and their word is consequently an authentic word. This is how it was with the Elder. It was his custom to embellish his words and occasionally his writings with a spiritual humor. In the Elder's humor there was nothing far-fetched, sensational, or clamorous. In essence his humor consisted of intelligent, dexterous and appropriate word-play and comments, which, on the one hand, were instructive, and, on the other hand, made the conversation with him a source of spiritual productivity and true refreshment.

Whenever conversing with theologians, the Elder would ask with his characteristic smile: "How do you theologians say this?" Or, "How do you understand this other thing?" Thus, removing himself from the group of theologians, he would teach us younger men not to call ourselves "theologians" and not to offer easy and absolute answers to difficult theological problems, particularly in the name of our "theological" diplomas.

At a festive dinner, speaking to the students and wishing to emphasize how important it is for our life to seek after God, he said: "I am envious of you and I marvel at you because you have found God. Poor me, I am still searching to find God."

On another occasion, when he was speaking about prayer, he said: "When I was on Mt. Athos and read from the Psalter during the sacred Services, my mind would often wander. Sometimes I would look out of the window to admire the flowers and the beautiful grape arbor filled with grapes, and I would lose my place where I was reading in the Book of Psalms. I tried to concentrate my mind on prayer, but it was distracted by nature, nevertheless. But, you know," he would add with a twinkle in his eyes, "God was good on Mt. Athos, He was not angry with me."

***

This, in broad and inadequate terms, was the holy Elder as I was blessed to know him. A man truly in love with the love of God, with the peace of God, with the truth of God. A man who loved prayer, and who practiced humility and simplicity in all things. A man who loved nature, loved to study and wanted always to learn. A joyful yet thoughtful man who also had a sense of humor. He was truly a man of God. A saint whose passing through this life was "a fragrant offering, a sacrifice acceptable and pleasing to God" (Phil. 4.18). This is why a little boy of five years, who came one day with his parents to the chapel of the Holy Cross, told his mother with excited enthusiasm: "Mother, I want to come here for Church, where that elderly *pappou* is celebrating." "Why my son?" the mother asked. "Because during the Liturgy I could see a beautiful light on his head."

Humanly speaking we have become orphans, holy *Geronta!* Our pain is great. But we are not discouraged. We know that in the end "you will not leave us to be orphans." It is not possible for your infinite love to abandon us. You have left us in the body, but not in the spirit. We shall communicate through prayer and the memory of your holy presence will always be alive in our thought, in our soul and in our heart. We ask for your intercession, O holy man of God, that other contemporary saints may be raised up in the Church of America, so that the river of holiness may irrigate the barren souls of men. This way Orthodoxy may grow deep, strong roots in the New World. May your memory be eternal, holy *Geronta.* Give us your blessing. Amen.